Praise for *Better Days*

Better Days offers practical wisdom for busy educators navigating life's challenges. Whether readers are looking to cultivate inner peace, manage change, or foster a classroom culture of mindfulness and presence, this timely guide offers short, digestible readings that inspire reflection and action in just a few minutes each day. Lisa Lucas's approach is compassionate, warm, and deeply personal, encouraging readers to embrace authenticity, vulnerability, and the simple joys of life. This book isn't just about self-improvement; it's about creating a ripple effect of kindness and positive change. Highly recommended for educators, caregivers, and anyone committed to improving their well-being and making the world around them a better place—one day at a time.

—**Dr. Marc Bertrando**, superintendent, Garnet Valley School District

Better Days is the perfect nightstand book, offering a short reading for every day of the school year. Each day's reading includes a quote (the sources of which range from the usual great minds to the less expected); a powerful reflection on the quote; and a suggestion for application in school. A great way to start or end the school day.

—**Dr. John Collins**, creator of Collins Writing Program

Better Days is a gift from an author who knows her field and her audience well. Dr. Lisa Lucas combines powerful research, poetic insights, and practical guidance in a collection that is sure to be off your shelf more than on it.

—**Stephen Hurley**, founder and chief catalyst, voicEd Radio

At a time when students' social-emotional health is in crisis, teachers need support—both to help their students and to prevent their own burnout. Seasoned teacher, coach, and consultant Lisa Lucas knows that teacher well-being is essential for student well-being, and in *Better Days* she offers research-based practices to help educators and learners form those small daily habits that increase attention, presence, and contentment in their daily lives. This book is a must-read.

—**Dr. Vicki A. McGinley**, author of *Parents and Families of Students with Special Needs*

In *Better Days*, Lisa Lucas provides practical and time-honored approaches to declutter and enrich our lives from the inside out. This is the best possible time to read this important book.

—**Dr. Bonnie Botel-Sheppard**, cofounder, Penn Literacy Network

Better Days

ASCD MEMBER BOOK

Many ASCD members received this book as a
member benefit upon its initial release.

Learn more at: **www.ascd.org/memberbooks**

Better Days

180 CREATIVE PRACTICES AND DAILY CONNECTIONS FOR TEACHERS AND STUDENTS

Lisa J. Lucas

ascd

Arlington, Virginia USA

2800 Shirlington Road, Suite 1001 • Arlington, VA 22206 USA
Phone: 800-933-2723 or 703-578-9600
Website: www.ascd.org • Email: member@ascd.org
Author guidelines: www.ascd.org/write

Richard Culatta, *Chief Executive Officer;* Anthony Rebora, *Chief Content Officer;* Genny Ostertag, *Managing Director, Book Acquisitions & Editing;* Bill Varner, *Senior Acquisitions Editor;* Mary Beth Nielsen, *Director, Book Editing;* Miriam Calderone, *Editor;* Georgia Park, *Senior Graphic Designer;* Valerie Younkin, *Senior Production Designer;* Kelly Marshall, *Production Manager;* Shajuan Martin, *E-Publishing Specialist;* Christopher Logan, *Senior Production Specialist;* Kathryn Oliver, *Creative Project Manager*

PAPERBACK ISBN: 978-1-4166-3348-8   ASCD product #125013
PDF EBOOK ISBN: 978-1-4166-3349-5; see Books in Print for other formats.
Quantity discounts are available: email programteam@ascd.org or call 800-933-2723, ext. 5773, or 703-575-5773. For desk copies, go to www.ascd.org/deskcopy.

ASCD Member Book No. F25-1 (Jan 2025 PSI+). ASCD Member Books mail to Premium (P), Select (S), and Institutional Plus (I+) members on this schedule: Jan, PSI+; Feb, P; Apr, PSI+; May, P; Jul, PSI+; Aug, P; Sep, PSI+; Nov, PSI+; Dec, P. For current details on membership, see www.ascd.org/membership.

Library of Congress Cataloging-in-Publication Data
Names: Lucas, Lisa J., 1964- author.
Title: Better days : 180 creative practices and daily connections for teachers and students / Lisa J. Lucas.
Description: Arlington, VA : ASCD, [2025] | Includes bibliographical references and index.
Identifiers: LCCN 2024041903 (print) | LCCN 2024041904 (ebook) | ISBN 9781416633488 (paperback) | ISBN 9781416633495 (adobe pdf) | ISBN 9781416633501 (epub)
Subjects: LCSH: Teacher-student relationships. | Mindfulness (Psychology) | Affective education. | Teachers—Conduct of life. | Students—Conduct of life.
Classification: LCC LB1033 .L73 2025 (print) | LCC LB1033 (ebook) | DDC 371.102/3—dc23/eng/20241017
LC record available at https://lccn.loc.gov/2024041903
LC ebook record available at https://lccn.loc.gov/2024041904

34 33 32 31 30 29 28 27 26 25   1 2 3 4 5 6 7 8 9 10 11 12

*This book is dedicated to
my granddaughters, Lucy May and
Lainey Anne LaRose. May you both
spread your love like wildflowers,
so that your presence helps others
have better days.*

Better Days

Introduction

You are never given a wish without also being given the power to make it true. You may have to work for it, however.

—Richard Bach

The original draft of this book was not specifically geared toward teachers and students. The book you hold in your hands began as a daily writing ritual during the COVID-19 pandemic. I would write reminders to myself of how I wanted to show up in the world despite the challenges we all were facing—strategies to stay present and purposeful and prevent getting overwhelmed. What people say is true: You write what you need to learn, and I needed daily reminders to stay present, positive, and optimistic about the future. (I still do.) Many parents, caregivers, and educators at the time were struggling to find activities for children who were stuck at home, and several contacted me for ideas. My background in education as an elementary school teacher and my research on well-being and stress reduction at the West Chester University of Pennsylvania, combined with the presentations I'd given on "Practices to Cultivate Presence," meant my areas of study and expertise were suddenly in demand.

So I began connecting what I was writing about to children as well because I knew the need was great. How many times have you been in a store and seen a child holding their mom or dad's phone, mesmerized by some game or video? I can't be the only one who sees children everywhere glued to a device rather than looking around and engaging with the world. Go into any restaurant and I guarantee you'll see kids looking down at a device, and their parents doing the same thing. In my heart, I know that any adult or child can benefit from the practices discussed here.

Better Days offers 180 daily social-emotional learning–focused readings and activities to help teachers and students navigate this epidemic of distractions and lost connections while integrating healthy habits into their lives. An underlying premise of this book is that we solidify and extend our own knowledge by teaching what we learn to others, and that the most effective way to do so is by being fully present and available in each moment. Presence cannot be taught; we simply must *be* present. We can then transmit our state—our way of being—to our students.

I used to wake up every morning and write in my calendar how "blah" I felt on a scale of 0 to 10. I was looking for patterns, trying to find exactly what was triggering that blah feeling that I couldn't seem to shake. Eventually, I figured it out—and that's what I share in this book: ways to get rid of the blahs and feel a bit better.

These days, I write down how *content* I feel from 0 to 10. I have found that life is much better when I am intentional about how I live my life. I try to be thoughtful about what I do first thing in the morning, the amount and types of media I consume, the food and beverages I put into my body, how much movement and fresh air I get, what's on my calendar, who I spend my free time with, what I read before bed, how much sleep I get, and more. Most important of all, I am intentional about my thinking. The practices in this book are intended to help you, too, slow down and consider your choices, behaviors, and thoughts.

Notice that I'm not calling this book a recipe for *happiness*. I have read countless self-help books, listened to endless podcasts on well-being, written courses on social-emotional learning, held retreats, written a book titled *Practicing Presence*, meditated and exercised daily, and begun every day with green juice—and I still have bad days. That's called life. But I have learned that with the right beliefs, thoughts, and actions, better days are possible. So while I am not going to claim that *Better Days* is the key to a blissful life—if only that were true!—I do believe it can make your life (and your students' lives) *better*. We can be aware of how we are feeling and intentionally do something to change our mindset.

I am a teacher, consultant, and therapeutic coach. All these roles overlap, but I've written this book from the perspective of a coach. Teachers teach and consultants try to fix things; by contrast, a coach mobilizes your inner resources to enhance your personal development, tapping into what you already know but may have forgotten and helping you gain clarity. Coaching ensures that changes are not just theoretical but mapped out with a clear, actionable plan.

I'd like to think teachers prepare students for life, not just to contribute to the global economy. The student activities in this book are all focused on social-emotional learning and can be continuously implemented both inside and outside the classroom. To prevent students from requiring interventions in the second decade of their lives, I believe we should help them as much as we can in the first decade. And we do this best by demonstrating: As teachers, we need to authentically show that the words we use and the actions we take matter. Never forget that our students are watching.

In *Write for Your Life* (2022), author Charles Wheelan notes that "the purpose of writing is to accomplish something" (p. 2). What matters is not how elegantly we write but whether what we write inspires people to take action. For this reason, I've tried to avoid jargon and excessive academic references in this book. Little of what I present here is especially original; for the most part, I have taken my research and translated it into practical daily entries for the reader to reflect on. As you read each entry in this book, I encourage you to share what you learn through discussion and activities with your students and, if time allows, with colleagues. My hope is that *Better Days* will supply you with what Irish poet and philosopher John O'Donohue, in conversation with *On Being* host Krista Tippett, referred to as "conversations… that sing in your mind for weeks afterwards":

> When is the last time that you had a great conversation, a conversation which wasn't just two intersecting monologues, which is what passes for conversation a lot in this culture? But when had you last a great conversation, in which you overheard yourself saying things that you never knew you knew, that you heard yourself receiving from somebody words that absolutely found places within you that you'd thought you had lost, and a sense of an event of a conversation that brought the two of you onto a different plane, and then, fourthly, a conversation that continued to sing in your mind for weeks afterwards? (Tippett, 2008)

Such conversations can expand and change lives, often in ways you will never know. Every day, we have 24 hours to live; *how* we live is up to us. We can live in a way that brings peace, presence, and joy to ourselves and others. This book's lessons serve as reminders that better days are only possible in the present moment.

How to Use This Book

A writer should write to their audience, and one thing I know about teachers is that many of you feel overwhelmed and overextended. You have too much to do and not enough time or support. You may not feel valued. Your students are distracted.

I have tailored this book to support busy teachers who are looking for daily guidance. Dedicating just a few minutes a day to the entries in these pages will allow you to embrace each day with a sense of hope and inner wisdom. This is a book you pick up when you need some inspiration or an idea for an inspiring classroom activity. Because I know how busy you are, the daily readings in *Better Days* are designed to be read in about two minutes. They don't need to be read sequentially; just open the table of contents, find a theme that interests you, and pick an exercise. You can then decide for yourself whether you want to try out a practice for yourself or implement it with students. Take what you read and do what you always do: make it work for you and your students. And if you miss a day, a week, or even a month of entries in this book, no worries—you can pick your reading up again at any point.

The format is simple. Each day's message includes a **topic** related to presence. This is followed by a **quote** or an **affirmation** strategically selected based on the intersecting connections it has to the topic. Next, a short passage of **research** or **reflection** related to the topic provides an authentic perspective on presence. These ideas are then followed with **practices** for teachers and **student connections** to try with learners.

There are endless possibilities for ways you might customize the use of this book to meet your needs. As a teacher, I don't want to be told what to do or how or when to do it, so I don't want to tell you those things, either. Instead, I want to provide you with ideas, resources, and examples and let you take it from there.

When everything feels like it's speeding up, the perception of time famine prevents many of us from enjoying sustained periods of daily reading and reflection. Think of this concise and practical book as a framework of daily practices that can be integrated into the frenetic pace of modern life—simple thoughts to anchor each day, carrying you through tumultuous challenges and ever-changing demands on your focus, energy, and time.

The following anchoring principles are intentionally threaded throughout this book:

- Teaching, learning, and living are all connected.
- Presence is a continuous practice—a way of living, not an end goal.
- Reflective personal inquiry is how we begin to initiate changes in our lives.
- We can't teach presence unless we practice presence ourselves.
- Better days are always possible.

Each entry is short, practical, and supported by research on behavioral science regarding positive change (Clear, 2018). This research shows that "microchanges" are the best way to establish new habits—but forming new habits requires practice. *Better Days* provides a practice for every day of the school year meant to instill positive habits that research shows can cultivate well-being. Yes, there will always be more to do than you can do, and there will always be more people who need and want your time than you can serve. Making smart choices is what matters, and one of the smartest choices you can make is to support your and your students' well-being.

As a teacher myself, I have always been drawn to daybooks. Something about wisdom distilled into a few words to bookend our days with thoughts of presence feels right to me. Starting the day with a short passage related to presence helps me notice more of the good and appreciate what's right in front of me. More time spent being present makes it more likely that I can bring forth my most flexible and resilient self.

There's no "right" time to implement the practices. You might choose to read a passage at home and then reflect on how you might incorporate what you read into your school day during your commute. You might practice first thing in the morning or save it for the end of the day. Some practices are meant to be done over a longer period, so you might select one and revisit it throughout the week. You might also choose to read a passage at night, then try the practice in the morning. What we put into our mind right before we go to sleep seeps into our unconscious mind.

I encourage teachers to use this book in a *personal* learning community that focuses on teacher well-being. Teachers could be given time to explore the readings and practices and then discuss them with colleagues. This is also an ideal book to give new teachers and their mentors at induction so they can learn together. This book is a springboard that could lead to meaningful conversations about teaching, learning, and living.

Bear in mind that the primacy/recency effect means students are most likely to remember the things they learn first or last in a sequence (Castel, 2008). The student connection activities in this book can be used with students as minilessons during morning meetings, closing circles, or any other time you and your students need to feel restored:

- Using these activities first thing in the morning ensures students begin the day with hope and pointed toward presence, which helps foster a collaborative environment conducive to learning.

- After lunch and recess, students benefit from restorative activities that transition them into the afternoon. Several of the activities in this book can be used to harness students' attention during a post-break slump and prepare them for the next academic segment of their day.
- To ensure students leave school for the day with a mindset that nurtures self-acceptance and promotes compassion, consider using the activities in this book as end-of-the-day practices. When parents ask their children what they did at school, they often share what happened last, so closing with these activities could spark meaningful conversations in the home. (Indeed, this book is also a helpful resource for parents.)

For the most part, the activities in *Better Days* are screen-free; it is essential for students to spend time away from devices if they are to be fully present. More than ever, today's students need opportunities to mingle with their peers in person and interact with skilled teachers who can facilitate respectful and well-intentioned discussions. Teachers can model discourse, perspective taking, and how to agree to disagree appropriately.

Of course, your choices about implementing the activities in this book will be informed by the age of your students. Older students could be given a topic as a prompt to write about, and younger ones could be provided with a journal in which to illustrate their reflections. Many of the activities can also be completed orally. When sharing material with students, you may choose to read the book aloud or summarize the contents. Some students might benefit from hearing how you've applied the practices into your life.

This book is designed to cultivate the habits and routines that will protect our passion so that we have the presence to provide quality social-emotional support to our students. This is as important as grading papers, attending committee meetings, and writing lesson plans. I would argue that it's actually *more* important. This book might help you remember why you went into education in the first place and what your priorities are. It can rekindle your passion and purpose.

One thing is certain: If you simply skim through this book without actively trying out any of the activities, little will change. But if you take action on what you read in these pages, not only will you change the way you look at things, but the things you look at may also change. Our thoughts, words, and actions create our world.

1

Attention and Intention

Your days don't have to happen at random.

All day long, we make decisions that affect how our days go. Some of these decisions are conscious, but many are not. The practices in this first chapter are meant to help you move through each part of your day with focused attention—but first, it's important to consciously set an intention as to how you want to show up for yourself and your family, friends, colleagues, and students.

Where Attention Goes, Energy Flows

Begin noticing and being careful about keeping your imagination free of thoughts that you do not wish to materialize. Instead, initiate a practice of filling your creative thoughts to overflow with ideas and wishes that you fully intend to manifest. Honor your imaginings regardless of others seeing them as crazy or impossible.

—Wayne Dyer

There's an old saying in journalism: "If it bleeds, it leads." This means that the more horrific something is, the more likely it is to draw attention. Unfortunately, the same is often also true in our day-to-day lives: negativity commands our attention more than positivity. This is largely due to the limbic system in our brains, which is constantly on alert for threats to our well-being. To retrain our brains so that we no longer focus so much on the negative, we need to consistently—not just once or twice, but every day—scan the environment for what is *good*. Sustained positive thinking "can stimulate the growth of new neurons and strengthen existing neural pathways associated with happiness and well-being" (English, 2024, para. 2). Positive thinking also "triggers the release of dopamine, often called the 'feel-good' neurotransmitter" (English, 2024, para. 3).

Practice

If you want good things to come your way, try to notice more of the good around you and carefully guard your internal commentary on the not-so-good things you see. You can become intentional about what you notice, but it takes practice.

Student Connection

Have your students go outside and spend a few minutes taking in their surroundings. Ask them to write down what they notice. Then, direct their attention to specific items or locations and ask them to write down what they notice about those specific things. Discuss the differences between what they noticed on their own and what they noticed when they were prompted to look at certain things. Most likely they will have noticed more details in the second case. Elaborate on how they might focus their attention and the benefits of doing so.

Focused Attention Meditation

Whatever we focus on and think about most becomes the strongest thing in our lives—for good or for ill.

—Hyrum W. Smith and Richard Winwood

Meditation is all about choosing where we place our attention. Is your attention scattered or focused? All too often, our attention is scattered when it should be focused on what brings us the health, joy, relationships, and results we want.

Practice

Find time to meditate today. There is no need to look at this as something you need to commit to for the rest of your life. Just make the time for two 4-minute sessions of practice. We build the habit of sustaining our attention one moment at a time.

Student Connection

Guide your students in a brief body scan. Use some variation of the following language:

Today we are going to practice moving our attention throughout our bodies, starting at the top of our heads and moving all the way to our toes. Practicing moving our attention helps us to get better at focusing and can help us relax and be ready to learn!

Focus all your attention on the top of your head. Squeeze all the muscles in your face nice and tight. Squeeze, squeeze, squeeze! And release.

Focus your attention on your shoulders. Squeeze all the muscles in your shoulders and arms. Squeeze, squeeze, squeeze! And release.

Continue down the body, squeezing and releasing. Ask students what they notice about their bodies and minds after completing the body scan.

Paying Attention

The moment one gives close attention to anything, even a blade of grass, it becomes a mysterious, awesome, indescribably magnificent world in itself.

—Henry Miller

There is a reason we often refer to *paying* attention: because we literally pay for it with our effort. The amount of sustained attention we typically pay to freely chosen tasks ranges from about 5 minutes for a 2-year-old child to a maximum of around 20 minutes in older children and adults. And this is for freely chosen tasks, not the types of tasks students are forced to pay attention to in school. Rarely do students get to choose what to focus on in class. This is unfortunate, because focusing attention is a skill that students can learn and improve on through regular training and practice. Madore and Wagner (2019) caution that "media multitasking"—the process of toggling between different media streams such as text messages and email—impairs memory. In reality, "multitasking" just means alternating between doing different tasks badly.

Practice

How many times have you misplaced your keys? In the mornings, do you search for your coffee cup even though you just set it down? It's not that you've lost these things; it's just that you weren't paying attention when you last had them.

Spend today really trying to pay attention to your daily tasks. Notice where you put your keys; slow down and think about where you are placing your coffee cup. Try not to get distracted. Do one thing at a time when possible. Avoid multitasking.

Student Connection

My colleague Jenny uses the flashlight as a metaphor for attention. When students are in charge of their "attention flashlight," schoolwork and learning become easier. Jenny conducts the following exercise to help make this point to students:

Bring a flashlight or laser pointer and shine it in various places in the room. Have students notice how they can track the light by paying attention to where it is. Ask your students to focus their attention flashlights on various things around the room. Ask them to notice how they are in charge of where they point their flashlights and for how long.

Attentive Listening

The quieter you become, the more you are able to hear.

—Rumi

Listening to outdoor soundscapes, particularly in spring, can help train us to become more present listeners.

Practice

Go outside and take a moment to tune in to the sounds around you. Don't listen too intently; just let the soundscape that emerges guide your focus.

One of my favorite practices is to go outside and simply listen to the wind. It's often in the background, unnoticed. The same is true of many aspects of conversation: the pauses between words, the sighs that signal exhaustion, the subvocalizations that aren't meant to be commented on. Try to notice these things when you speak with others.

Student Connection

Have your students sit outside and tune in to the sounds they hear. Say, "If you hear a bird, notice the pauses between the chirping. Do other birds echo their sound? Do you think they are communicating? Can you name a bird by its sound?" If there are no birds in the area, have students truly listen to anything they can hear. Then, have them share and compare, noticing that we all tune in to different sounds.

The Art of Inner Listening

All of humanity's problems stem from man's inability to sit quietly in a room alone.
—Blaise Pascal

Sometimes we just don't know what to do or where to go. Making decisions by ourselves can feel daunting. One strategy for overcoming this lack of clarity is to practice the art of inner listening. We tend to be surrounded by external distractions, and most of us don't spend enough time in quiet solitude. The internal teacher that dwells within you—not your ego, but your wise self—is worth listening to. As the saying goes, "Be still and know."

Practice

The next time you must make a decision, take a moment to eliminate external distractions, ask your inner self what to do, and wait for the response. If you wish, you may write your question in a journal and then record the response. What's most important is to quiet the mind, so do whatever it takes to achieve stillness. I often find stillness when I go for a walk, as my mind tends to settle when my body is moving.

Student Connection

As teachers, we need to gently guide young students to listen to their own inner voices. In their book *Hold On to Your Kids*, Neufeld and Maté (2006) address the unprecedented parenting challenges posed by the rise of digital devices and social media. By helping to reawaken instincts innate to us all, the authors empower adults to be what nature intended: a source of contact, security, and warmth for their children. Inevitably, students are going to find themselves in situations where they're tempted to make a choice that could harm them or violate their values. We want them to have a strong "internal teacher" encouraging them to do the right thing.

To help students recognize the importance of listening to their inner voice, share stories about times when you chose to listen to yours. During morning meetings, cultivate a safe space where students feel comfortable disagreeing with one another. Set clear rules: Everyone gets a turn to talk and has equal airtime; everyone listens to everyone else's ideas; no put-downs allowed. Encourage students to express their opinions and to back them up with a strong "why."

Schedule Time to Think

It is not enough to be busy. The question is: what are we busy about?

—Henry David Thoreau

We should not need permission to pause and think, as doing so is necessary for our creativity to flourish. Rather than seeing "thinking time" as something you only get when you've done everything else, make it a priority. Spending time connecting the dots leads to breakthroughs, so be a dot collector. Everything you read, listen to, or watch and everyone you talk with is a dot on your radar. Expand your mind and welcome new ideas and perspectives to ensure the dots connect far and wide.

Practice

Schedule some thinking time this week. Mark it on your calendar. Turn off all your distractions—no dings, no buzzes, no chimes. This is a time for silence.

I like to pair thinking time with walking. This is a time to recalibrate, to adjust goals and priorities. If possible, go outside during this time to walk and think. You'll find you are more refreshed and focused when you return.

Student Connection

One of the simplest ways to give your students more time to think is to increase the wait time after you pose a question. Studies show that the length of a teacher's pause after asking a question positively correlates with student learning, yet teachers typically wait less than one second after asking a question for a student response (Rowe, 1986). Further, after a student stops speaking, the teacher follows up with another question in less than one second. Believe it or not, pausing for three or more seconds showed a noticeable improvement in learning.

Today, when you pose a question in class, try to pause for 5 to 10 seconds before calling on a student. Notice if you have more volunteers than usual and if the quality of their responses has improved.

Less Wired, More Connected

Every status update is just a variation on a single request: "Would someone please acknowledge me?"

—Marc Maron

I want to be more connected to humans than to things that need to be charged or plugged in. Over the years, I've replaced a good deal of social media with an intent to connect with others face to face and listen to them deeply. I'm especially eager to connect with strangers, like the woman around my age who bags the groceries at my local supermarket. Is she happy? Are those worry lines, or is she just tired? When I thank her for her help, she looks surprised to be acknowledged.

Practice

Can you eliminate social media from your life for a week? How about a day? If so, what will you do with your newfound time?

Student Connection

Challenge your students to abstain from electronic media for a week. Children and students rely on us to set boundaries with electronics, so set them. Although devices such as tablets can be helpful in the classroom, they can also quickly become an issue. Plan a week of tablet-free activities. See if you notice a difference in your students' engagement when electronics are not involved in any lessons. Have them journal about what they do after school without TV, internet, or video games. This may be the most difficult homework assignment of their lives!

Notice More

The ability to be in the present moment is a major component of mental wellness.

—Abraham Maslow

As the world speeds up, it's important for us to decelerate—to be present while the world is distracted, to enjoy the small moments, to do one thing at a time. When we go too fast, we make mistakes. When we slow down, we tend to notice more. We can practice presence as we walk, sit, drive, shower, and so on—all the things we normally do, except with a focused awareness of what we are doing.

Practice

Today, concentrate on water. Every time you encounter water, give your full attention to it—how it looks, feels, tastes. Let water remind you to focus, slow down, and tune in. Use water as an opportunity to notice more.

Student Connection

We often ask our students to pay attention, but we first need to teach them how to do it. Have your students go outside and each find a small pebble. Ask them to get a sense of their pebble by examining it closely with their eyes and hands. Have them all put their pebbles in a circle, then mix them up and see if they can each find their pebble. Next, you could have them see if they can distinguish their pebble from others with their eyes closed.

Flow

I just go with the flow, I follow the yellow brick road. I don't know where it's going to lead me, but I follow it.

—Grace Jones

In an interview with *Wired* magazine (Geirland, 1996), famed psychologist Mihaly Csikszentmihalyi offered this explanation of flow: "The ego falls away. Time flies. Every action, movement, and thought follows inevitably from the previous one, like playing jazz. Your whole being is involved, and you're using your skills to the utmost" (para. 2). Numerous factors signal the experience of flow, including complete concentration, the fact that the activity is intrinsically rewarding, feelings of serenity and a loss of self-consciousness while being absorbed in the activity, and a sense of timelessness that involves feeling so focused on the present that you lose track of time passing (Csikszentmihalyi, 1990).

Practice

What is something you can do today that you love but that's a bit of a challenge? Whether it's running, gardening, writing, painting, sewing, or anything else, set a goal, eliminate distractions, and give yourself 15 minutes to just do it. This exercise is linked to increased levels of satisfaction and self-actualization (Dhiman, 2007). Notice how you feel during those 15 minutes.

Student Connection

Achieving flow requires that an activity be at a level of challenge just above one's current abilities. If a challenge is too hard, students will become anxious and give up; if it's too easy, they'll become bored. Give students assignments that fall into the sweet spot. To make sure work feels relevant to their lives, provide them with choices (including hands-on activities for those who learn best that way). Consider ways you can give students more opportunities to make, create, and explore.

Discuss flow with your students. Have them think of times when they have become really absorbed in something. Ask, "What were you doing? What did it feel like? How long were you absorbed? What helps you stay focused? What gets in the way of being 'lost' in something? What are you doing when you lose track of time?" Make sure to highlight activities that don't require electronic devices.

2

Authenticity

When our words and actions convey authenticity, our students trust us, and when they trust us, they take risks and freely engage in learning without the fear of being wrong or different. Throughout this chapter, you will find practices and student connections focused on aligning your actions with your core values and beliefs. The practices will help you take stock of your own authenticity; the student connections are windows of opportunities to open up discussions with your students.

Be Who You Are

Be yourself; everyone else is already taken.

—Oscar Wilde

Being authentic and true to yourself is the best gift you can give yourself and others. When we worry about what others will think, we're second-guessing our own true nature and short-changing both them and ourselves. Why would we do this? It may stem from our early childhood experiences; if we weren't valued for being ourselves, if we twisted ourselves up into knots to receive approval from our caregivers, a pattern may have developed that has become an unconscious way of life. Luckily, we can change this pattern by developing an awareness of our actions.

Practice

Place a hand on your heart and take a few deep, grounding breaths. Vow that today you will notice whenever you adjust yourself to the people around you. Recognize when you are "turning it on" to be accepted by others. Take a risk and share something vulnerable about yourself with someone you trust, or choose a theme song that sums up who you are and play it for them.

Student Connection

Talk with students about how their value is not dependent on the positive regard of others. Social media often portrays a false image of people and events. We want to teach children to be inner-directed and authentic. Affirm to students that their value isn't dependent on physical qualities or achievements. They don't need to earn approval; they are valuable just the way they are.

Have your students choose a theme song that speaks to them.

Read David Shannon's *A Bad Case of Stripes* (1998) with students to help focus on the theme of being true to oneself. Have students create a self-portrait with stripes drawn across their face, and have them define what each colored stripe can teach others about them.

Inner Freedom

Knowing others is intelligence; knowing yourself is true wisdom.

—Laozi

Inner freedom means marching to the beat of no drum but your own and listening primarily to the still, small voice of your wise inner self. It means being bold enough to do what you feel is right regardless of what others think. It means not trying to figure out what other people expect or how you can best fit in.

Practice

Think about the people who like you just the way you are—the ones who truly get you. If you don't have people like that in your life, start looking for them. They are out there, and guess what? They want to find you, too. But you must be yourself for them to find you.

List five words that describe who you are. If you haven't yet found "your people," start looking for those same characteristics in others.

Student Connection

The best teachers are the ones who allow themselves to be human in front of their students, and one way to do this is to show your more lighthearted side. In your classroom, establish random "silly times"—brain breaks that encourage silliness. The rules of silly time: don't worry about what other students think, have fun, and be yourself.

Imperfection Beats Impersonation

It is better to do your own duty, however imperfectly, than to assume the duties of another person, however successfully. Prefer to die doing your own duty; the duty of another will bring you into great spiritual danger.

—Krishna, quoted in the Bhagavad Gita

If we strive for anything, it should be authenticity. Instead of trying to emulate others, living up to some standard of perfection, we should be ourselves. Who we are is good enough.

When my daughter realized one of my granddaughter's eyes might need correction, she smiled, thinking of how adorable she would look in glasses. The need for correction wasn't a deficit; it was just one part of the magnificent, beautiful girl she already was.

Practice

We are living in a culture that promotes impersonation—impersonating someone thinner, smarter, more successful, or simply better. Not true. Who you are with all your imperfections is perfect.

Student Connection

Share and discuss the following story from *The Art of Possibility* (2007) by Rosamund Stone Zander and Benjamin Zander with your class:

> A little girl in second grade underwent chemotherapy for leukemia. When she returned to school, she wore a scarf to hide the fact that she had lost all her hair. But some of the children pulled it off, and in their nervousness laughed and made fun of her. The little girl was mortified, and that afternoon begged her mother not to make her go back to school. Her mother tried to encourage her, saying, "The other children will get used to it, and anyway your hair will grow in again soon." The next morning, when their teacher walked into class, all the children were sitting in their seats, some still tittering about the girl who had no hair, while she shrank into her chair. "Good morning, children," the teacher said, smiling warmly in her familiar way of greeting them. She took off her coat and scarf. Her head was completely shaved.
>
> After that, a rash of children begged their parents to let them cut their hair. And when a child came to class with short hair, newly bobbed, all the children laughed merrily, not out of fear, but out of the joy of the game. And everybody's hair grew back at the same time. (p. 164)

Try Softer

It's dark because you are trying too hard. Lightly child, lightly. Learn to do every-thing lightly. Yes, feel lightly even though you're feeling deeply. Just lightly let things happen and lightly cope with them. So, throw away your baggage and go forward. There are quicksands all about you, sucking at your feet, trying to suck you down into fear and self-pity and despair. That's why you must walk so lightly.

—Aldous Huxley

The science of effort brings good news for idlers everywhere: Trying too hard really is counterproductive. Growing up, many of us were drilled to always work harder, give 110 percent, don't slack. In his book *The Inner Game of Tennis*, W. Timothy Gallwey (1997) notes that trying too hard to succeed at things can actually interfere with our own natural learning capabilities. Instead of forc-ing things, we can trust the intuitive wisdom of our bodies and reach a state of relaxed concentration.

When things don't go the way I want, I tend to try harder. But I'm slowly learning to "try softer" instead.

Practice

Think about a part of your life where you are trying too hard. See if you can release the pressure a bit and instead try and experience flow—a state we can't achieve through force.

Can you remember something you enjoyed doing when you were a child that you haven't done as an adult? It might be time to try that activity again, especially if you are feeling a bit stuck. Today, rather than push and persevere, try to soften and relax.

Student Connection

We usually teach students that hard work always pays off. However, it's just as important for them to understand that being fully present and enjoying our-selves can also help us be more productive (and is much more satisfying).

Young children are often in a natural state of flow during unstructured play time. Our job is to provide them with opportunities to discover and create. Such opportunities help them identify activities that they truly love—ones during which they can lose track of time and focus on process rather than the end product.

Your Wise Self

Listen to the wind; it talks. Listen to the silence; it speaks. Listen to your heart; it knows.

—Ojibwe prayer

Your wise self is the part of you that is always encouraging you, always in your corner. Your wise self has confidence in you. When you listen to your wise self, you feel no guilt or doubt.

Practice

Use images or words to describe this wise inner part of you. Take a moment to be still. Reflect on what your wise self wants for you. Before you make decisions today, ask your wise self what's right for you. By doing this, you are training your mind to get in touch with—and trust—your most intuitive self.

Student Connection

If we can teach students to recognize the importance of listening to their own inner voices rather than seeking the approval of others, they'll be better equipped to make wise and healthy choices. This is a skill that is best learned early, when decisions don't have as many potential repercussions.

Explain to students that they have an "inner owl" they can rely on to make smart choices. Provide them with a template of an owl and have them customize it however they want.

If you don't already have a peace corner in your classroom, create one—a space where students can take a moment to pause, be quiet, and center themselves. Post the students' owls at the peace corner.

Don't "Should" on Yourself

My teacher once told me, "No one is perfect… that is why pencils have erasers.

—Mahesh Bhatt

I should have eaten healthier. I should have exercised. I should have worn sunscreen. I should have learned how to sew. I should have been a better wife, mother, daughter, niece. Our inner critic never stops, but is full of commentary about how we have not done enough, have not been enough, are not enough. Try not to "should" on yourself. Catch yourself and notice when you say *should*.

Practice

Follow these three steps to quiet your inner critic and feel in control of how you think about yourself:

1. Cultivate awareness of your thoughts. Awareness is necessary for change.
2. Stop and redirect your thoughts. Quietly listen to the sounds around you for 20 seconds. Notice what you see and smell. Forget your inner critic and ask instead what your wise self wants for you.
3. Reframe and talk to yourself as you would to a friend.

Continually practicing these small actions will gradually help you stop "shoulding" on yourself.

Student Connection

When you hear your students "should" on themselves, have them follow the preceding steps while modeling how to reframe self-critical thoughts. Don't overpraise your students, but make it clear you value their efforts. Intentionally compliment their hard work to another adult and allow them to overhear it. Our students are always watching and listening.

Your Name Is a Song

Your name is a golden bell hung in my heart. I would break my body to pieces to call you once by your name.

—Peter S. Beagle

We don't often think about how our parents chose our names, but it stands to reason that they gave it some thought. I've always been fascinated by nominative determinism, which is when a person's name fits their calling or purpose in life (e.g., a baker named Baker, a writer named Wordsworth). At least one study suggests that we may even look like our names: When asked to guess which of a handful of names corresponded to a photograph of a person's face, both humans and computers were able to do so correctly more often than mere chance would suggest (Zwebner et al., 2017).

Practice

Find the meaning of your name. For example, when my daughter was choosing a name for her soon-to-be baby girl, she learned that Lainey was the French form of Helen, which is either from the Greek *helene*, meaning "torch" or "light," or *selene*, meaning "moon." The torch is a common emblem of both enlightenment and hope. Metaphorically, light is used as a symbol of extreme goodness or joy. The moon signifies wisdom, intuition, birth, death, reincarnation, and spiritual connection.

Consider whether you are living up to your name. If not, what changes could you make?

Student Connection

Have your students find the meaning of their name or research the story of why they were given their name. A great homework assignment is for them to interview their parents or caregivers about how their names were chosen. Have students write or "dot" their names in rainbow colors (or whatever design they choose), tracing the letters over and over, either outside using sidewalk chalk or inside using paints, markers, or watercolors. You could also write letters on interlocking blocks and ask students to "build" their names.

Avoid the Second Arrow

In life, we can't always control the first arrow. However, the second arrow is our reaction to the first. The second arrow is optional.

—The Buddha

If we could accept ourselves as we are, that would be monumental. If we could accept what life hands us, that would be the beginning of peace. Easier said than done, of course, but we can at least work toward these goals.

The opposite of acceptance is resistance. Often, we resist what is happening in the present moment if it's something we haven't planned for or find undesirable. But resistance doesn't help in such instances; in fact, it often makes things worse.

There is a Buddhist parable called Two Arrows about dealing with suffering more skillfully. The Buddhists say that any time we suffer misfortune, two arrows fly our way. The Buddha explained: *Picture yourself walking through a forest. Suddenly, you're hit by an arrow. The first arrow is an actual bad event, which can cause pain. But it isn't over yet. There is a second arrow that brings more pain and suffering. The second arrow represents our reaction to the bad event. It's the manner in which we choose to respond emotionally. We can learn to avoid the second arrow.*

Practice

Watch for those first and second arrows today, then examine how to replace the second arrow with first aid in the form of a cooling-down exercise like the one described in the following section.

Student Connection

Explain to students that emotions are physical sensations that can be gently released. If your students are old enough to understand the analogy of the two arrows, share it with them and ask them to recall times when they experienced the "second arrow." Incorporate some simple movement and breathing exercises, such as the Stair-Step Breath exercise: Take little steps of breath through the nostrils as though you are climbing a mountain—three to six inhalations until your lungs are filled. When you reach the top of the metaphorical mountain, imagine something beautiful. Say "peace" to yourself and then imagine taking a glass elevator down the mountain as you release the breath through the nostrils.

Trusting Your Own Inner Voice

What you seek is seeking you.

—Rumi

There comes a time when you need to stop listening to the online courses, the YouTube videos, and the well-intentioned advice of friends. Instead, you need to trust yourself. Ask and really listen for an answer. Surrender to your wise self.

It can be challenging to trust the answer we receive. It might not be the one our rational mind wants. It may not seem logical. Trust it anyway.

Practice

Our bodies can often guide us. Try out this simple practice: Stand with your feet about two fists' distance apart. Close your eyes, then ask a yes or no question. If your body sways forward and backward, the answer is yes; if it sways side to side, it's a no. Experiment with this process. The ability to concentrate on the question, block out external stimuli, and focus allows clarity to emerge.

Student Connection

One of the greatest gifts we can give our students is the ability to trust themselves and not succumb to peer pressure. It's crucial that we give them a solid foundation in discerning right from wrong. We teach this more through our actions than our words.

Show students how to ask, listen, and trust their own inner wisdom. Encourage them to trust their instincts and listen to their inner voice.

Training Intuition

What lies before us, and what lies behind us, are tiny matters compared to what lies within us.

—Ralph Waldo Emerson

Intuition is the sudden consciousness of previously subconscious information. The word *subliminal* means "below the normal threshold of conscious awareness." You can enhance your intuition by consistently asking your subconscious to tell you what it knows that your intellect doesn't.

Practice

We all experience intuition differently. Some may see images in their mind's eye; for others, intuition may be a physical sensation (the classic "gut feeling"); still others have a more emotional response. Writing down words and phrases as they come to you when considering a problem may also provide you with a different perception. Slow down and notice how or where you experience intuition.

Recall a time when you trusted your intuition over someone else's opinion. How did that turn out? Now, recall a time when you mistrusted your own intuition and trusted someone else instead. What was the result?

Student Connection

You have an opportunity to teach students to look inward and get in touch with their thoughts and feelings. Intuition means having "mindsight"—a type of internal education that builds awareness and can be helpful in making decisions. To strengthen students' intuition, guide them to ask themselves these questions:

1. What was my gut reaction?
2. Do I have a hunch about this?
3. How do I feel when I think about *X* situation?
4. Does this seem like the right answer/the right thing to do?
5. Where in my body do I notice a reaction?
6. If I did know the answer, what would it be?

Wiser or Weaker?

Into each life some rain must fall.

—Henry Wadsworth Longfellow

What if we have been given exactly the circumstances required to develop our unique gifts? Too often, we begrudge the cards we've been dealt rather than focusing on the good that can come out of difficult situations. University of Wisconsin psychologist Shilagh Mirgain (2020) found that up to 70 percent of people experience positive psychological growth from difficult times, such as a deeper sense of self and purpose, a greater appreciation for life and loved ones, and an increased capacity for altruism, empathy, and acting for the greater good.

Practice

Reflect on any gifts you may have cultivated out of a difficult experience. Are you wiser or weaker as a result of the challenge you faced? If wiser, have you supported others with what you've learned? As you go about your day today, consider how you can use your gifts to support others.

Student Connection

Ask your students to list three difficult circumstances they've faced in the past month and think about any good that came from them. How could they use what they've learned to become stronger, smarter, and more resilient?

To extend this activity, turn it into a Think-Pair-Share. After students list their difficult circumstances, have pairs share and discuss what each learned from the situation.

The Right Moment

If a train doesn't stop at your station, then it's not your train.

—Marianne Williamson

Timing is everything: When the time is right, things fall into place effortlessly. But when we push to have things occur on a particular timetable, struggle tends to ensue.

So, we wait, sometimes patiently, usually anxiously, wondering all the while: When will the future bring me what I long for?

Let go of the longing and simply tune in to the present moment, knowing that if what you want is meant for you, it will emerge when the time is right. Practice patience.

Practice

Today, stop pushing and manipulating outcomes. Good things will happen at the right moment, and they will happen naturally.

Student Connection

When talking about waiting for the right time with students, use the analogy of a cat waiting to pounce at a mousehole. The cat is very patient and still, springing into action at just the right moment. Remind students that timing counts for a lot, and sometimes they just have to keep trying. They might not get exactly what they're planning, but their perseverance will pay off in the long run.

Don't Settle

What you want exists—don't settle until you get it.

—Author unknown

Most of us can think of someone who settled for less than they deserved: a friend who stayed with a partner who did not truly meet their needs, or a colleague who worked for lower compensation than they merited. Often, these are people who we would normally think of as strong self-advocates. But when you think about it, many of us have settled for less at some point in our lives; it's only when we finally move on from the situation that we are shocked by how long we've put up with it.

So why do we settle? Often it is because certainty feels more comfortable than uncertainty. However, the truth is that there is no such thing as certainty. Even our current situation will eventually change. Perhaps it's worth reframing the limiting beliefs that keep us stagnant and taking a leap into the unknown. Only you know if it's worth the risk, but at least consider the possibility that something more is waiting for you.

Practice

Think deeply about what you genuinely want. What is most important to you? Think about your job, your relationships, and your aspirations. What would you change today if anything was possible? Answering these questions honestly is the first step to contemplating change. This isn't a plug for the perpetual search for more or better. Staying in a situation isn't always bad; perfection isn't possible, so don't overlook the good that's right in front of you. Remember that those Instagram stories and Facebook photos only show the good. Only you know if you've settled for less when you truly deserve more.

Student Connection

Children start picking up cues about their perceived worth at an early age. As teachers, we have a tremendous responsibility to make sure every student knows their worth. We want to teach them to love and respect themselves.

Invite students to close their eyes as you read to them from the book *All the Places to Love* (1994) by Patricia MacLachlan. Ask them to visualize what the story describes as they listen. After finishing the book, have students draw people, pets, or places that make them feel absolutely loved for who they are.

Affirmation Flags

Affirmation: I am worthy of the safety that allows me to be soft.

—Kierra C. T. Banks

Affirmations are intended to affirm the truth about you—to highlight a quality about yourself that you're aware of but don't always confirm. Daily positive affirmations help you believe in yourself and reinforce what you're capable of achieving. You can say them aloud, write them down, or post them somewhere visible to serve as reminders.

Practice

I keep a deck of affirmation cards. When I need affirmation, I randomly select one of the cards and vow to live up to what it says. For example, one morning, I drew a card that said, "I have the ability to direct my own thoughts." My bedtime card read, "I will never get there, so I will enjoy my journey." It's a fun exercise that I've found to be more effective than making one up to say to myself in the mirror, when I'm not always in the best frame of mind to believe it.

Student Connection

Provide students with flags made of cardstock that have "I am _____" written on them and have them complete the sentence. Each flag could be a different color, and when students are done you can string them together for display in the classroom.

Every Monday, post a new affirmation on the classroom door. Have students pause as they walk into class and whisper it to themselves. On Friday, give students their own copy of the affirmation to take home and hang somewhere in their home. Students can write affirmations about their classmates as well.

Regrets Can Help Us Course Correct

Never regret. If it's good, it's wonderful. If it's bad, it's experience.

—Victoria Holt

Life is a series of choices and paths not taken, so it isn't unusual to feel regret over some of our decisions. However, regret can keep us stuck. It often entails feelings of disappointment, guilt, or remorse about the past and can divert us from the joys of the present moment. Accept that you may have regrets, and use any regrets as valuable information to guide you to make better choices in the future.

Practice

Find a picture of yourself at the age of the students you are teaching. What would you like to tell this child? Instead of regretting past mistakes, forgive yourself for anything you've done wrong, knowing that at the time you were doing your best.

Student Connection

Share younger pictures of yourself with your students. Talk about your likes, hobbies, and dreams at that age. Share a few things that you regret doing when you were young and all the things you are proud of at your current age.

Encourage students to bring in a photograph of themselves from a few years prior. Have them share both regrets and accomplishments with their younger self.

Be Vulnerable to *Be*

You'll never know who you are unless you shed who you pretend to be.

—Vironika Tugaleva

There is nothing so freeing as being completely yourself with another human. However, that takes mutual trust and a feeling of safety. Too often, we worry how others may see or judge us if they knew the real us. But to be your true self, you need to show your entire self. You can't just pick and choose the one side of yourself you want to show.

Practice

Identify a few individuals you are comfortable with and display your vulnerability to them. The goal is to be and show your true self. Notice how your vulnerability affects the relationship.

Student Connection

Brené Brown (2018) defines trust as "choosing to risk making something you value vulnerable to another person's actions" and distrust as "deciding that what is important to me is not safe with this person in this situation (or any situation)." Although we want to encourage our students to be themselves, it's also important for them to understand they must be discerning about whom they trust.

With your students, create a T-chart showing signs that someone is trustworthy (e.g., you feel safe sharing deep feelings with them) versus signs that they are untrustworthy (e.g., if you show them a vulnerable side of yourself, they laugh or gossip about it to someone else).

3

Change

Everything in life is in a constant state of flux. Many of us educators have experienced the cyclical nature of school our whole lives, since we were students ourselves. For most of us, this means we go through some kind of change each year. Because some of these changes are imposed on us, we can release control, accept the changes, and even embrace them: Think of the way we look forward to meeting a new group of students every school year.

But in our personal lives, we often resist change, choosing to remain with the familiar rather than leap into the unknown. Getting out of our comfort zones can be uncomfortable because—let's face it—uncertainty is a bit scary. As you read this chapter, the goal is to begin to see change as an opportunity rather than a loss. The practices will give you chances to embrace the unfamiliar and nudge you to grow and explore unchartered territories—and the student connections will help you lead learners through the same process.

Choose Change

When in doubt, choose change.

—Lily Leung

Change is the one constant we can count on in life. Are you someone who appreciates change, or would you rather things stay the same? Of course, we don't have a choice in the matter. When my kids were young, I would sometimes wish they would stay that age forever, thinking things couldn't possibly get better. Not true. Things may change, but in every present moment there exists the opportunity for "bests."

Practice

Notice what you are holding on to a little too tightly. Do you wish holidays were the way they used to be when your children were young? Maybe it's hard to watch your parents age, and you wish you could turn back time. Often, we wish teaching was the same as it was a decade or more ago. Can you lighten the grasping and holding, and in letting go, find more time to appreciate the present? When we let go, new possibilities for what can be will have the space to emerge.

Student Connection

Children can have a hard time with transitions. Teach students that embracing change can lead to wonderful new opportunities. For example, every new school year brings possibilities for new friends.

Have students make a list of all the friends they've made each year since they were old enough to have friends. If a student has difficulty generating a list of friends, have them list peers they would like to be friends with or qualities they might look for in a friend. You could also ask students to write down the things they will be able to do in future grades that they can't do now.

Let All Things Be Exactly as They Are

Nothing comes ahead of its time, and nothing ever happened that didn't need to happen.

—Byron Katie

I'm often torn between letting all things be exactly as they are and the desire to make things better. What if we can do both? Let things be as they are but experience them in a way that brings acceptance to the situation, an internal peace resulting in better days.

Practice

Trying to be at peace with things as they are while also wanting things to improve can feel like walking a tightrope. Sometimes, the best action is nonaction. When we accept things as they are, we paradoxically allow things to shift; acceptance is not the same as resignation or passivity. Instead, it allows things to evolve without pushing so hard. It can be easier to accept something unwanted when we explore the opportunities and possibilities that come from it.

Endings, such as the loss of a job or the end of a relationship, are good times to practice the process of acceptance. Sometimes endings arrive when we're not prepared, and they remind us that so much in our lives is beyond our control. What we *do* control is the way we handle endings, which can shape what happens next. When faced with an ending, take stock of how you feel. Does your body get tight or tense? Do you feel anxious, sad, or apprehensive? Is your mind busy remembering, suppressing, or planning?

Student Connection

Toward the end of the year, an activity called the Web of Life is a good way to provide closure for your class while demonstrating connection. Have students sit in a circle. Holding a ball of yarn in your hands, share one significant thing about your time together as a class. Then throw the ball of yarn to someone else while you hold on to the end piece of yarn. The person you've thrown the yarn to then shares, and the process repeats until all students have shared. At the end, when everyone is holding their part of the yarn, point out to your students that even though your time as a class is ending, you are still connected in a friendship web, as shown by the yarn you're all holding. Explain to students that they will continue to create these webs of personal connection throughout their lives.

What Would Your Future Self Say to You?

Your future self is watching you right now through your memories.

—Aubrey de Grey

Gary Chadwell of Collins Educational Associates used to close his professional development workshops with a letter-writing activity. He would ask participants to summarize what they had learned from the workshop and identify three main strategies they would be implementing with their classes. Then he'd pass out envelopes and ask participants to place their letters in them, seal them, address them to their own homes, and hand them back to him. A few months later, he would mail the letters back to everyone. Receiving the letters was a great reminder of what we had learned and planned to put into place in our classrooms.

I've replicated this exercise with professional learning groups countless times. One of my favorite variations is writing a letter to my future self in which I describe what I plan to be doing 12 months from now. For example: "Dear Lisa, way to go! You published your book, have passed Level 3 of your therapeutic coaching program, and still managed to keep your promise to incorporate more leisure into your life."

Practice

Write a letter to your future self describing all that you've accomplished this year, then make a calendar reminder to read it six months from now. When you read it, I guarantee it will redouble your desire to meet your goals. You can reread the letter throughout the year as a reminder of your priorities.

Student Connection

Encourage students to write a letter to themselves about their hopes and dreams, either academic or personal, for the year ahead and return it to you. Make a promise to mail each student their letter one year from now. Alternatively, have students write the letter at the beginning of the year and return it to them on the last day of school.

There's Always a Choice

No matter what the situation, remind yourself "I have a choice."

—Deepak Chopra

We always have choices, even if we tend to forget that. When we are feeling stuck or trapped, we resort to using language such as "I have to." The truth is, we *choose* to, often either out of obligation or guilt. As adults, we have endless choice when it comes to how we spend our time. How we use our time is a clear indicator of our priorities.

Practice

When you're feeling stuck, list all the possibilities and alternatives in front of you. Don't commit to a choice; simply brainstorm. Then, step away from the situation and go focus on something else. Come back to your list the next day and see if any of your possibilities has potential. If so, you've taken the first step toward more freedom.

Student Connection

Use the classic games of musical chairs and tic-tac-toe to illustrate the concept of choice to students. Musical chairs illustrates making decisions quickly: If you don't pick a chair and move to it quickly, you will lose. With practice, children learn how to choose, asking questions like *Is the best chair the nearest one? The one with the fewest people around it? Facing me or facing away?* This activity is also a great way to practice losing, an important skill many students need some guidance in. Often parents haven't allowed their children to lose when playing games, so it could be a new experience for younger students.

Tic-tac-toe takes a more tactical approach. Not only do students need to get a row of three, but they also need to prevent their opponent from getting a row of three. It takes a lot of concentration and practice to get good at this game, and it can be tough at first for young children, but they will soon catch on. This game can help children learn to take turns, regulate their emotions (especially when they lose), and think flexibly.

Transformation

Embrace each challenge in your life as an opportunity for self-transformation.
—Bernie Siegel

Whatever we want to transform, whether it's our physical health or our mindset, we need to pace ourselves to do it. If we take things too slowly, we run the risk of quitting because we don't see enough progress soon enough to stay engaged. If we go too hard and too fast, we run the risk of giving up due to fatigue or burnout. It can be difficult to gauge the right amount of effort it takes to make sustainable positive change in your life. Consistency and accountability are key. Having an accountability partner is helpful. My role as a coach is often to help others keep their pace practical and their goals attainable.

Practice

Choose just one thing you'd like to transform. A key element in transformation is intention, so write down the outcome as if it has already happened. Chart your progress daily or consider an accountability partner or coach to help you stick to it.

Student Connection

Transforming anything requires awareness. Ask your students to close their eyes and think about something inside them they'd like to transform—maybe they are afraid to raise their hand, for example, or anxious of making a mistake. Next, teach them to identify the opposite of their fear and to strive for that. For example, the opposite of being afraid to raise their hand is being brave enough to risk it. What they are really asking is to transform their fear into bravery.

It's Not Too Late

Tell me, what is it you plan to do with your one wild and precious life?

—Mary Oliver

If you're reading this, it's not too late.

We always have choices, even when it seems like we don't. That's what it means to be an adult—to be faced with endless choices. Even if we can't quit our day job, we can still pursue other interests or careers, taking one step at a time in the direction of our dreams while still getting the bills paid. I've always had a core job that provided benefits and a stable income that I supplemented with outside pursuits to feed my soul, like coaching, speaking engagements, and writing this book.

Practice

If money and time were no object, what would you do with your "one wild and precious life"? What are you passionate about? For now, how can you incorporate those interests into your daily life? Start small, knowing that the more time you spend on what you truly love, the likelier it is to blossom into something bigger than you could have imagined.

I recommend reading the book *When You Wonder, You're Learning* (2023) by Greg Behr and Ryan Rydzewski. It has insights and practical advice from thinkers, scientists, and teachers, including many who worked with Fred Rogers of the classic children's program *Mister Rogers' Neighborhood*.

Student Connection

Adults often ask children, "What do you want to be when you grow up?" Let's see if we can improve on that question. First of all, they want to "be" themselves. The question also implies there is one set final occupation they should commit to. No wonder kids often dread this question. Instead, ask questions about their interests: "When does time seem to fly by?" "Is there something that you're curious about and would like to explore more?" "What do you think you're good at?" After listening to their answers, you could tell them about jobs that you think might interest them.

Questions That Could Alter Your Life

Change your thinking, change your life.

—Feather Stone

The moment we ask a question, we begin to change.

Inquiry is a kind of intervention. Poet David Whyte has spoken about the art of asking beautiful questions—ones that ask us to reimagine ourselves, our world, and our part in it. One question he posed at a talk I attended was "Can I be quiet, even inside?"

Practice

Imagine it's two years from now and your life is better than you could ever imagine. Who do you spend time with? What do you do for fun? Where do you live? What type of work do you do? Consider writing your responses in a journal.

You might also reflect on this list of my top five coaching questions:

1. Is this what you're meant to be doing?
2. What do you really want?
3. When do you feel most valued?
4. What is your body trying to tell you?
5. What do you need to let go of?

Student Connection

Post the following questions at stations around the classroom:

- Who makes you feel good when you spend time with them?
- What is your favorite activity to play inside?
- What is your favorite subject in school?
- What are you worried about?
- What would you like your parents to do more of?
- What do you like most about yourself?

Next, place students in pairs and have each pair choose which question or questions they would like to explore. After they've discussed the question or questions, reflect as a whole class. Are there any changes they could make in their lives based on their answers? You can also use these questions as writing prompts or conversation starters during morning meeting.

Making Decisions

I am not a product of my circumstances. I am a product of my decisions.

—Stephen Covey

In his 2015 book *Driven to Distraction at Work*, Edward M. Hallowell offers a series of structures to help with decision making. Following is my summary of the processes he suggests along with some of my own suggestions:

- Make a list of all the possible choices and rate them on a scale from 1 to 10.
- After compiling the list, write the pros and cons of each one.
- Brainstorm with a friend, then list the choices in order of priority.
- Make a list of the most likely possibilities and display it where you will see it each day. Let it percolate in your subconscious until one choice emerges as the lead contender.
- Give yourself a deadline to make a decision.

Practice

If making a decision is too overwhelming but not too pressing, give yourself space to ignore it until you decide on a strategy to address it. When you are busy running these things over in your mind all day, you are not being present. Often the answer will come when you release the pressure of constant thought. Even if you are not actively thinking about your decision, your mind is subconsciously working on it.

Another strategy is to write all the possible choices on separate sticky notes. Crumple up the notes, then choose one at random. Notice how you feel when you read it. Most decisions are best made from an inner knowing, and this process helps you to acquire that clarity. It also helps to speak your decision aloud; hearing the actual words can incite an inner reaction.

Student Connection

Show your students a picture of an ant and a picture of an elephant, then ask them which they would rather be and why. This is a great decision-making activity for students that helps build their thinking and reasoning skills. You can also offer some variations like "Would you rather be a baby or an adult?" "Would you rather be a frog or a kangaroo?" "Would you rather have extra hands or extra feet?" or "Would you rather go camping or visit a beautiful city?"

Processing Memories

The difference between false memories and true ones is the same as for jewels: it is always the false ones that look the most real, the most brilliant.

—Salvador Dalí

I was going through my old journals recently and wished I could hug the 8-year-old who wanted her parents to stay married, the teenager hyperfocused on her weight, the college student so unsure of which career path to pursue. Eventually I drove to a remote park and threw the journals into a dumpster. I was afraid someone else might read those raw and unfiltered memories.

I'm not sure I'd have the guts to write as candidly today. Someone snooped in my journal once, and ever since then I've been more guarded when I write. I'm working on changing that.

In reading my old journals, I realized how inaccurate our memories are; the way I remember many events didn't line up with my own written record. Research shows that our memory doesn't work like a video camera; instead of recording and then accurately replaying an event, our minds create a mix between our current life and what we are remembering, inserting details from the present into the memories we retrieve from the past (Paul, 2014). The purpose of journaling is not just to produce a written record for our future selves, but also to help us process our experiences in the moment.

Practice

A memory that elicits negative feelings is one that we have yet to fully process and learn from. Ask yourself what you need to learn from the event so that you can fully release any trapped emotions. Notice if seeing the memory from a new perspective makes you feel different.

Student Connection

Journaling should be a part of every school day. Homemade personal journals are wonderful creative outlets for students to draw and write, but there is always the risk that others could read them. Imagine if every student could have an ongoing digital journal that they could write in at school and that no one else could ever access.

Consider having your students end every school day with a journal entry. You might ask them to summarize what they learned about themselves that day.

Embrace Impermanence

No man ever steps in the same river twice, for it's not the same river and he's not the same man.

—Heraclitus

Although I grasp the reality of impermanence—trust me, I've read and written about it—I'd be lying if I said I've learned to accept it. I'm still trying, but when things I love come to an end, I almost always have that yucky feeling in my stomach.

The way to address this, of course, is to keep practicing acceptance of the present moment. Notice how good things, bad things, and things in between all come to an end. We waste so much time trying to hold on to the good rather than being fully present.

Practice

Notice when you're holding on too tightly to things and not allowing them to just be. It's in the noticing that we can bring awareness to our grasping and practice letting go.

Student Connection

Share the 1982 book *The Fall of Freddie the Leaf* by Leo Buscaglia with students. The story is about a leaf named Freddie and how he and his companion's leaves change with the passing seasons, finally falling to the ground with winter's snow. Use the example of Freddie and the seasons changing to lead a discussion. Ask students, "What other sorts of things change? Are changes good or bad?" This can be an especially good conversation to have either at the beginning or at the end of the year, when students are in a phase of transition.

Identifying Coping Strategies

Things do not change, we change.

—Henry David Thoreau

Think back to your childhood. What coping mechanisms did you use when your immediate needs weren't met? How do those same coping skills show up in your life now?

As a coach, I have found the Enneagram—a framework of nine established, interconnected personality types—to be a comprehensive, integrative system for accelerating self-knowledge and supporting positive change. It is a powerful tool that helps us understand our motivations, our core beliefs, and the unconscious patterns that drive our behavior—as well as understand why others behave the way they do. The Enneagram helps me understand how my clients approach their challenges and which fears, beliefs, and emotional and behavioral patterns are most prevalent in their lives. Most important, it reveals their greatest potential.

Practice

Read about the Enneagram and, for a small fee, consider taking the Riso-Hudson Enneagram Type Indicator (RHETI) self-assessment at https://www.enneagraminstitute.com. Although there are alternative free Enneagram self-assessments, I've found this one to be the most accurate and informative.

Student Connection

The True Colors Personality Test was created by Don Lowry in 1978 using the colors blue, orange, gold, and green to categorize the strengths and weaknesses of most young people. I've used this test with students and gotten valuable insights about how they cope with obstacles. You can find numerous free versions of this test online; one that works well for younger students can be found at https://microsite-sws-prod.s3.amazonaws.com/media/editor/24/TrueColors PersonalityTestfreebie.pdf.

When reading stories with students, call attention to how the various characters cope with problems, and then brainstorm alternative ways of handling the situations. We want to teach students that there are often multiple ways to meet our needs—some healthy, some not so healthy.

Just a Little Bit Better

If today you are a little bit better than you were yesterday, that's enough. And, if tomorrow you are a little bit better than you were today, then that's enough.

—David A. Bednar

When you are not feeling great, you can always turn your attention to something that feels just a little bit better. If you can focus on something positive, your perspective changes, which can change your energy. Have you ever noticed that when things start to go wrong, if you don't change your state, even more things go wrong? If you can focus on what's going right, you will attract more things that are going right.

Practice

Even a slight change of state can alter your outlook. If your present state—the internal pictures, sounds, feelings, self-talk, and behaviors you are using—are creating unwanted responses, shift your mind to think about the desired state that you'd like to achieve. It can be hard to cut through fuzzy thinking and get clarity about what you really want. Sometimes it helps to slow down, close your eyes, and see what emerges when you ask yourself, "What is it I really want?" and then write the response down. If time allows, envision what will change if you get what you really want.

Student Connection

Learning is state-dependent; it can be hindered when learners feel anxious or incapable. Ask your students to remember a time when they had difficulty learning something and have them describe how that felt. Then have them reflect on a time when learning was fun and easy. See if they can determine the similarities and differences between the two experiences, perhaps using a Venn diagram. Help them to identify what makes learning just a little bit better for them. These are the differences that make all the difference.

Making Friends with Anticipation

The first week of August hangs at the very top of summer, the top of the live-long year, like the highest seat of a Ferris wheel when it pauses in its turning. The weeks that come before are only a climb from balmy spring, and those that follow a drop to the chill of autumn, but the first week of August is motionless, and hot. It is curiously silent, too, with blank white dawns and glaring noons, and sunsets smeared with too much color.

—Natalie Babbitt

Educators often start to anticipate the beginning of a new school year when August arrives. This is when we most need to learn to be present and avoid wishing the last days of summer away. However, if we can't keep ourselves from planning, it can be productive to do a few small tasks each day.

Practice

For some of us, it can be helpful to start making some small preparations for the new school year during the summer. Rather than feeling overwhelmed by all that needs to be done, dedicate a few hours to preparing. Once we start something, we can realize it's doable, even pleasant, to do. Whenever we anticipate that something will require a lot of work, it's best to take small steps toward completing it rather than perpetuate the anticipatory anxiety.

Student Connection

The beginning of the school year is both an exciting and a challenging time for students and teachers. The anticipation students feel about the year ahead can bring a variety of emotions.

At the end of the school year, have your students write letters to themselves for next year. Have them include their favorite parts of this school year, what they are looking forward to in the next grade, and anything else you think would benefit them. Have students address the letters to their homes, then mail the letters back to them a week or two before the new school year begins, when their level of anticipation will be at its highest. Feel free to include a handwritten note from you as well.

Shift Your Focus

If you shift your focus from yourself to others, extend your concern to others, and cultivate the thought of caring for the well-being of others, then this will have the immediate effect of opening up your life and helping you to reach out.

—The Dalai Lama

Has a conversation ever changed your life? Don't ever underestimate the power of a connection—even a brief one.

Have you ever noticed in a coffee shop or restaurant that some customers never look at the server who takes their order? They might be on their phone, or just choosing not to engage with another human. What used to be considered rude is now the new normal. But by simply shifting our focus to others, we can learn more, become curious, and possibly think differently.

Practice

Engaging in conversations with strangers has many health benefits, including increased happiness, a greater sense of belonging, improved mental sharpness, a decreased sense of loneliness and isolation, and a stronger sense of trust. Research (Sandstrom & Dunn, 2014) has found that people who had brief conversations with their baristas or strangers during a morning commute reported having a more positive mood and a greater sense of connection than those who did not engage in such conversations.

Today, take a moment to intentionally converse with someone you may see often but don't really *know*. You have no idea what the impact might be; so many people feel alone, and sharing a "hello" can be a bright spot in someone's day.

Student Connection

Guide your students to strike up conversations with people they see often but rarely talk to (e.g., the bus driver, a cafeteria worker). Teach them that small moments matter and what we say to others can have a huge effect.

Many children are cautioned not to talk to strangers. Take some time to clarify the difference between a stranger and someone they see daily but don't know very well. Give students concrete tips to begin a conversation. They could introduce themselves, offer a compliment, ask the other person's opinion about something, or bring up something they have in common.

Have students tally how many times they smiled at someone today and had a smile returned.

Don't Let It Get You Down

There are only so many times you can allow someone to let you down before you will no longer tolerate being disappointed. When things go wrong between two people, something has got to give. You get to the point where you get tired of being the only one trying to fix things.... You've got to do what's right for you, even if it hurts.

—Brigitte Nicole

It's time we accept that some people can't give us what we need. We may have spent years trying to get their support when the fact is, they cannot or will not provide it. Let it go. Accept those individuals the way they are and release all expectations.

According to the author, coach, and podcaster Mel Robbins (2022), "There are three things about people we need to accept: (1) They would if they wanted to; (2) you can't make someone change; (3) stop being mad at people for not being who you want them to be."

Practice

Take stock: Is there anyone in your life who consistently lets you down? Release your expectations and you'll find you no longer feel so bad when others disappoint you. Cut the ties of hope and accept reality—they either can't or won't do what you want them to do.

Student Connection

Children understandably expect others, especially adults, to make amends when they've let them down. As teachers, we can model apologizing when we've fallen short and then follow the apology with a discussion. Through these candid conversations, children begin to realize there is always an opportunity to repair a mistake or to apologize for a wrongdoing, but not all adults will do this.

Giving students concrete strategies to use when they are feeling let down is helpful. One strategy is to "breathe the rainbow": Take deep breaths while thinking about your favorite things for each color of the rainbow. Another strategy is simply to play with modeling clay; something about the tactile experience of kneading and pounding the clay can help them work through their feelings.

Commit to Try

There's a difference between interest and commitment. When you're interested in doing something, you do it only when circumstance permits. When you're committed to something, you accept no excuses, only results.

—Art Turock

Trying something is much different than committing to it. But we can also commit to trying something, which doesn't mean we have to do it forever. The word *commit* may hinder us from taking chances, but we can commit for the short term. When I commit to something and I don't follow through, I feel like a failure. So instead, commit small, and success will usually follow.

Practice

What are you committed to? Is there something you'd like to learn more about, experience, or pursue? Look at your calendar right now and write in the two times you will focus on this activity. There is no need to look at this as something you need to fit in for the rest of your life. Just make the time to fit it in twice in the upcoming week. For example, I'm committed to walking 20 minutes a day as often as I can in the upcoming year. I'll begin by finding small gaps in my calendar this week that allow me to walk daily.

Student Connection

Begin by teaching students about commitment. A good story for this is Dr. Seuss's *Horton Hatches the Egg* (1940), in which a bird mom who is tired of sitting on her egg convinces Horton, an elephant, to sit on the egg while she takes a break. When her short break turns into a permanent absence, Horton is left to sit on the egg much longer than he'd anticipated. In the end, his commitment is rewarded with the hatching of a little elephant bird.

Design scenarios and have students take part in a line-up to vote on how committed the person in each scenario was: One end of the line stands for full commitment, and the other end stands for no commitment, with a spectrum in between. Here is an example:

Lisa begs for a piano and promises she will practice every day. She does practice, just not *every* day—more like right before her piano lesson.

4

Common Humanity

One thing most teachers have in common is that we feel
the effects of time scarcity. We feel as though our work is
never done; there is always more to do and not enough time
to do it. Our lives are busy, and we find ourselves endlessly
juggling tasks and attempting to ration our time and energy.
It can all feel overwhelming. When we're in touch with our
common humanity, though, we remember that the way we
feel is a shared experience. In all the ordinary moments
of our ordinary lives, the practices and connections in this
chapter remind us that we are not alone.

Uncommon Commonalities

The longer we listen to one another—with real attention—the more commonality we will find in all our lives. That is, if we are careful to exchange with one another life stories and not simply opinions.

—Barbara Deming

Have you ever felt like you didn't belong? This feeling is one I hear repeated from students in my classes at the university, among colleagues in my department, and from therapeutic coaching practitioners when talking about their clients' issues. Perhaps we're more alike than different, which suggests that we do belong after all.

Practice

In schools, in sports teams, and in all kinds of groups, there are students who naturally fit in and those who feel like outsiders looking in. These are known as low-status students, and they are everywhere despite often going undetected.

Structure your classroom activities to include students who are often overlooked or left out by their peers. Think about how you can pay more attention to students you usually pass over. Whom can you include rather than overlook? How can you make someone feel seen? Can you model ways to include everyone and exclude no one?

Student Connection

Break students into small random groups of four or five. Have them brainstorm and come up with something uncommon that they all have in common. It can't be that they are all a certain age or go to the same school; it must be something less obvious, such as having a favorite hobby or sport in common. Once they come to a consensus, have each group create a banner with their uncommon commonality written on it. At the beginning or end of every day, have the group members meet to clarify assignments, touch base, and generally support one another. The function may vary, but the group remains the same, and the intent is for everyone to be seen, acknowledged, and supported by their peers.

Look Up

Listen, are you breathing just a little, and calling it a life?

—Mary Oliver

Are you living each day, or are you just getting through it? Do you need some kind of spark to renew your love of life? Spending time in nature can remind us how magnificent life can be.

Practice

The next time you are in a crowded place, look around and notice how many people you see looking up. My guess is not many. As I walk across my college campus on the way to class, I see that most students have phones in hand and aren't aware of their surroundings or making eye contact. For most of our days, our focus is downward or straight in front of us. The next chance you get, go outside and look up at the sky. You might be surprised by how this simple act of changing your visual field will affect your mood.

Student Connection

At the beginning of every school year, request that parents send in a beach towel for their child and take your students on a mindful walk. Pause throughout the walk to look up. Ask them what they notice. Find a spot where students can lie down and gaze at the sky. I tend to wait until a day when there is a blue sky with puffy white clouds. When you get back to the classroom, give the students some blue paper and white paint or cotton balls and have them re-create what they saw. It's a great opportunity to teach students that our feelings are like clouds in the sky, ever changing, never permanent, and the sun is always somewhere waiting to shine.

We Have No Idea

Making it look easy is the hardest thing in the world to do.

—Sarah Ban Breathnach

Do you ever feel like other people have it made? I've been at the coffee shop at noon on a weekday and wondered why the people there weren't at work or how they could seem to be so at ease in the middle of the day. (Never mind the fact that I, too, am there!) I often make gross generalizations about others that may or may not be based in reality.

Practice

Imagine what someone would think about you if they saw you on a "good day." Then, list three hardships you have experienced in your life. Would anyone guess that you've experienced these challenges by looking at you? Notice the stories you tell yourself about others that perhaps are more fiction than truth.

Student Connection

Have your students write down some of the hard things they have experienced in their life. Tell them not to add their names so their responses will be anonymous. They can write as many things as they want. After everyone has written, have students gather in a circle. On the count of three, students throw their "hardships" toward one another. Most will end up on the floor. Each student should pick one, read it, and consider whether they'd prefer to keep it or trade it. Students often end up searching for their own hardship, realizing they'd rather have that than trade it for something unknown and possibly worse.

And That Too Am I

How far you go in life depends on your being tender with the young, compassionate with the aged, sympathetic with the striving, and tolerant of the weak and strong. Because someday in your life you will have been all of these.

—George Washington Carver

Abrams and colleagues (2006) found that the very thing we often avoid— interacting with those who are different from us—is one way we can bridge divides and increase empathy toward others. When we avoid people who are different from us, we miss out on opportunities to challenge stereotypes and recognize that, although different, we often share more characteristics than we realize.

Practice

Notice which characteristics annoy you the most in others. Now do some honest analysis: Do you share any of those characteristics? Usually, we find that we have at least a trace of those same characteristics that we try our best to conceal, so encountering it in someone else can quickly trigger us.

Student Connection

Fostering an appreciation of our common humanity is one of the best ways to prevent bullying and discrimination. One way to do this is to have students discover the many ways in which they are alike.

Read a series of statements and have students "pop up" or stand if it applies to them. For example, say, "Pop up if you ever forgot your homework" or "Pop up if you snore." Once students become familiar with this activity, you can have them create their own "pop up" statements.

Forming Connections

Everybody laughs the same in every language because laughter is a universal connection.

—Yakov Smirnoff

I asked my aunt with stage 4 cancer if she had any regrets. This is a woman who lived in a beautiful home that her architect husband had designed and built for her on one of the Finger Lakes. She said, "Both your mother and I cared about the wrong things. We cared about stuff when we should have cared more about people." Many people say something similar at the end of their lives. What truly matter are the connections you have with others.

Practice

The connections you form when you're fully present can make the difference between someone feeling truly heard or neglected. Most of us know what it feels like when someone barely pays attention to us. It can make you feel like you're not valued. The opposite—when someone gives you their undivided attention—tends to produce a sense of rapport and ease.

Today, give your full attention to everyone you interact with. When you talk with someone, really look them in the eye.

Student Connection

Have students trace the letters of a word on their classmates' backs and see if they can be present and attentive enough to decode it. (Younger students can draw shapes or single letters.)

You could also play a version of the game "I'm Going on a Picnic." Have students take turns saying an item they are going to bring to the picnic—but the catch is they also have to list all the items their classmates said before them. This exercise forces students to pay close attention to others while allowing them to have fun and be silly.

What You Have to Give Is Enough

It is the sweet, simple things of life which are the real ones after all.

—Laura Ingalls Wilder

There is someone out there who needs exactly what you have to give. Never think that what you have to offer is insignificant. You always have the potential to help someone else. I rarely know how much of a difference my suggestions make in the lives of others, but I do know that if anything I do impacts even one person, then it has value.

Recently, I was having a tough day, and I stopped by a friend's house. All she did was listen, but I left feeling supported.

Practice

What is one small thing you can do today that will provide solace or comfort to someone who needs it? If you approach your day with this mindset, the right person and the right situation will emerge.

Student Connection

Have students pick one another's names out of a basket and keep the name they select a secret. Tell them that for the rest of the month, they are to commit random acts of kindness for this student—simple acts like sharpening their pencils, leaving them a nice note, or offering them a healthy treat. The simpler the better, illustrating that whatever you have to give is enough.

Give and Receive Support

Anything is possible when you have the right people there to support you.

—Misty Copeland

There are so many ways to support others. Just knowing I have support available can be enough to make me feel better. I don't necessarily need anyone to do anything other than simply be there.

Take a moment to think of the ways you have supported significant people in your life. How have you provided them with support? How have they supported you?

Practice

Support doesn't need to be overt. When you are in a space of presence, others feel it and naturally gravitate to you. Your job isn't to fix or save anyone. If you are always offering solutions and giving advice, you are assuming others aren't capable of solving their own problems. Most people don't like listening to advice. Instead, be like a lighthouse, shining a light to guide them as they maneuver their own route.

Student Connection

At the beginning of the year, pair up your students with grade-level peers from a different classroom. Because students tend to share and converse more when they are immersed in an activity, have them do backpack interviews: Taking turns, each student shares something they have in their backpack while their partners ask who, what, when, where, and why questions about the item. The next time they meet, they might trace each other on butcher paper. At the end of the year, they can repeat the tracing activity to see how much they've grown. As the students start to connect with and know their partners, you might encourage them to think of each other as "safe buddies" they can count on for support.

Ask for Help

Remember, if you ever need a helping hand, it's at the end of your arm. As you get older, remember you have another hand: The first is to help yourself, the second is to help others.

—Audrey Hepburn

Think of all the ways you have supported yourself. Do you support yourself as much as you do others? Do you ask for support? Do you accept support? Don't be a martyr. If you need help, be direct, ask the right person, and allow them to help you without apologizing. Don't be ashamed of not being able to do everything yourself; wise people know when they need help. Be clear about what you need, ask, and then accept the answer. Let others choose whether to help or not; if they say no, be grateful that they were honest.

Practice

Let go of trying to do everything alone. Make a to-do list for the next two weeks and figure out where you might find help. When the time comes, ask for help, and don't apologize for asking. Be sure to notice whether you are able to accept someone else's way of doing things if it is different from yours.

Student Connection

Students need to know that there is always help available to them. Often, they aren't aware of the many resources at their disposal, whether inner resources or external supports. Tell your students that if they ever need assistance, all they need to do is ask and you'll be there. Those words can make more of a difference than you think.

Ask your students to meet in small groups and discuss why they think an adult would choose teaching as a career. Guide them to understand that most teachers choose the profession because they like to help others.

Look for the Helpers

When I was a boy and I would see scary things in the news, my mother would say to me, "Look for the helpers. You will always find people who are helping." To this day, especially in times of disaster, I remember my mother's words and I am always comforted by realizing that there are still so many helpers—so many caring people in this world.

—Fred Rogers

During difficult times, scanning for the helpers can change your perspective tremendously, from a worldview of hopelessness to a position of renewed optimism and efficacy. There are always helpers; we just have to look for them with intention.

Practice

Today, notice the helpers in your daily life: the customer service rep who helps you out on the phone, say, or the person who holds the door for you. When you start to focus on all the positive encounters you have during the day, you'll find they are everywhere.

Student Connection

For a week, have students use chart paper to keep track of anyone who helps them. At the end of the week, tally the results and predict what the results will be the next week. Conduct the same activity the following week and compare against the initial results. When we teach students to look for the good, they become more accustomed to looking for it and consequently notice it more.

The Fred Rogers Institute (2022) provides the following tips for helping children navigate potentially traumatizing new events:

- When the world feels uncertain... we can help children feel safe by letting [them] know we will always care for them and love them, no matter what.
- Be mindful of what children hear and see on the news. Children can overhear media and conversations that are not intended for them.
- Let children know you are always open to their questions.
- Let children know that their feelings are always safe with you, whether they are feeling worried, angry, sad, or anything at all.

Collaboration Versus Competition

Success is best when it's shared.

—Howard Schultz

I used to love competition—whether it was a sporting event, a job interview, or a chili cookoff, I was all for it. More important, I loved to win—but over time, competition lost its appeal. Nowadays, I'd rather collaborate and have everyone feel as though they've won. I think I finally realized that when we all rise, we all win.

Practice

Ask yourself in what ways you're competitive. With whom do you feel competitive? What's behind the competitiveness? Could you collaborate more and compete less? Today, try to share with your colleagues an engaging or effective lesson or strategy that has worked well with your students. I recall when my grade-level partner Diane shared her ideas of having a "book jacket fashion show" and an end-of-year reading challenge. I reciprocated by sharing some of my own ideas with her, and everyone benefited—especially students.

Student Connection

Explain to students that you can feel like a winner without making others feel like losers by supporting your peers rather than conspiring to be the best. Ask students to consider the benefits and drawbacks of winning versus supporting. Be honest and take stock. The world needs more collaboration, and while it's a skill that can be learned, it may need to be practiced.

To practice collaboration, have students arrange their chairs in two concentric circles, one inside the other, with the students in the inner circle facing those in the outer circle. Provide students with a problem-solving challenge and have the facing pairs discuss possible solutions. After students have shared, ask the students in the outer circle to move one chair to the right and discuss the question with a new partner. Continue for a few rotations until the class has heard numerous possible solutions. This exercise requires collaboration, listening skills, and possibility thinking.

Another activity students enjoy is having to rank the class from oldest to youngest, but *without any talking*. Students must work as a whole group to do this and can get very creative about sharing their age and birthday without speaking.

Audacity to Hope

Hope is being able to see that there is light despite all of the darkness.

—Desmond Tutu

Who doesn't need to hope? We all hope to be healthy and for our future to be bright. Let's remember to hope for others, too.

Practice

Think of someone you know you'll see today. When you're in their presence, think of what you would most hope for them. You don't have to say it aloud; they will feel it.

When we are struggling, typically one of two things occurs: We either remain hopeful or become pessimistic. Challenge yourself to be somewhere in between, accepting the everyday reality of the situation while staying positive.

Student Connection

Begin the year by introducing the following Responsive Classroom (2019) "hopes and dreams" activity, which I've been successfully using for years:

- Preview the year in some way. Perhaps you can share about activities, books, field trips, or science experiments students will experience in the months ahead.
- Brainstorm hopes and dreams with students.
- Allow time for students to share their hopes and dreams. They could do this verbally and follow up in writing or by drawing.
- Make students' hopes and dreams visible by putting up a display in the classroom.

Building Belonging

True belonging never asks us to change who we are. True belonging requires us to be who we are.

—Brené Brown

In his book *Belonging: The Science of Creating Connection and Bridging Divides,* Stanford researcher Geoffrey Cohen (2022) maintains that belonging is the secret to flourishing in an age of division. Cohen describes belonging as the feeling of being part of a group that values, respects, and cares for us. All of us know the feeling of *not* belonging, and few of us like it.

Practice

A culture of belonging starts with adults. In our schools or district, we can work together to foster an environment of caring, connection, and belonging. At your next faculty meeting, select one of the practices in this book and invite everyone to share. Notice who doesn't seem comfortable and make a conscious effort to involve them in some small way.

Student Connection

Students who report a higher degree of school belonging experience better mental health and are at lower risk of suicidal ideation (Boyd et al., 2023). They also perform better academically (Cai et al., 2023). Cultivating a sense of belonging for all students begins by integrating inclusive practices and providing opportunities for student voice and leadership. Greeting each student at the door is a simple way to ensure every student begins the day feeling seen.

You can also kick off a weekly All About Me ritual in which students introduce themselves to the class by sharing artifacts representing their lives and cultures. Each week, send the All About Me box (a decorated shoebox works well) home with a different student, who brings it back and shares their chosen artifacts. Teach your students inquiry-based stems to help them respectfully engage and ask questions such as "Can you tell me more about _____?" and "Where did you get _____?"

In the Muck

Before spring becomes beautiful, it's plug-ugly, nothing but mud and muck. I've walked through early spring fields that will suck the boots off your feet, a world so wet and woeful you yearn for the return of snow and ice. Of course, there's a miracle inside that muddy mess: those fields are a seedbed for rebirth.

—Parker Palmer

There will inevitably be times in your life when you feel stuck: you've lost your joy, you're devoid of feeling, you've got no interest in anything, your days don't feel purposeful. When this happens, it's important to remember that it won't last. When you're in the muck, it can be impossible to imagine you'll ever get out, but you will—trust. Ask for help and it will come—perhaps not on your timeline, or in the way you expect, but it will come.

Practice

If you're feeling in the muck, ask for support and know you're not alone. If you are experiencing symptoms that last longer than two weeks, seek the help of a professional. If you're not sure where to start, there are numerous mental health resources online, including https://www.nami.org/about-mental-illness/mental-health-conditions/depression.

Student Connection

According to the Centers for Disease Control and Prevention (CDC) (Bitsko et al., 2022), between 2013 and 2019, 9.8 percent of U.S. children ages 3–17 were diagnosed with anxiety problems, and among adolescents ages 12–17, 20.9 percent had experienced a major depressive episode. Here are some symptoms to look out for:

- Difficulty concentrating or completing assignments
- Seeming sad, tired, and uninterested in activities they've enjoyed before
- Frequent physical symptoms, like stomachaches and headaches
- Decreased self-esteem and increased risky behavior

Schools can help implement interventions and identify students who are experiencing systems of anxiety or depression. The CDC (2023) published a fact sheet to support this effort: https://www.cdc.gov/childrensmentalhealth/features/anxiety-depression-children.html.

Perfection Is Overrated

Perfection has to do with the end product, but excellence has to do with the process.

—Jerry Moran

Would you want to have a friend or partner who was perfect? I wouldn't. It would be a horrible reminder of all my own imperfections. Authenticity outranks perfection.

Practice

Write a list of three things that didn't go the way you had planned. Was the result life-altering? Did you gain anything positive from the experience? Looking back, would you do those things differently?

Student Connection

Have students complete a "Beautiful Oops" assignment, based on the book of the same name (Saltzberg, 2010). Give each student a piece of blank paper and ask them to scribble on their paper for four seconds. After they are done, invite students to write their names on the back of their papers, crinkle them up, and throw them into the center of the room. Have students pick up one another's papers and take five minutes to turn the scribble into a beautiful picture. Students then return each paper to its original owner. Discuss the importance of being able to turn an "oops" into something beautiful rather than throw it away.

Read *The Book of Mistakes* (2017) by Corinna Luyken to students. This book reminds us that the way we look at the world and ourselves is always a work in progress.

If You Really Knew Me, You'd Know That . . .

Vulnerable people are powerful people. Opening your heart and sharing it means you're going to get so much love in your life. And it's the way to true connection and real purpose and meaning in your life, in my opinion.

—Amy Poehler

At the beginning of the year, I give my college students the following sentence frame: "Dear Professor, if you really knew me, you'd know that _____." They have the option to complete the prompt in writing and submit it to be read only by me. My friend Alison originally shared the activity with me, and I've since shared it with countless colleagues as well. It's a good way to get to know my students and cultivate relationships.

Practice

Take turns completing the "If you really knew me" prompt with friends and colleagues. You'll be amazed by what you'll learn about people you thought you knew so well.

Student Connection

You can modify the "If you really knew me" exercise for younger students using these alternative prompts:

- The hardest thing I have ever done is _____.
- What I find most difficult about coming to school is _____.
- What I love most about school is _____.
- If I had three wishes, I would wish for _____.
- Most people see me or label me as _____.

An Ending for Everything

Sometimes the things that break your heart end up fixing your vision.

—Author unknown

How do we avoid mourning something wonderful that we know will pass all too soon? The key is to remain in the present moment. We never know what the next moment will bring, and if we spend time looking behind or looking forward, we miss what's right in front of us.

Practice

One of my favorite Laura Ingalls Wilder books is *These Happy Golden Years* (1943). In it she writes, "The last time always seems sad, but it isn't really. The end of one thing is only the beginning of another" (p. 158). That line has stayed with me. I've personally experienced the loss of relationships, jobs, and even the lives of loved ones, all of which I've mourned in different ways.

Endings are never easy. If you really care about someone or something, to see it end hurts your heart. Saying goodbye to students at the end of the year can be a bittersweet experience. I always close my class by giving everyone the option to say a few words thanking the class for the time spent together.

Student Connection

Several years ago, at the beginning of class, 1st grader Dave whispered in my ear, "Mrs. Lucas, Clyde died." Clyde, as I and everyone else in the class knew, was Dave's dog. I asked him if he'd like to talk about it with the class. He nodded his head. We gathered in our customary circle to begin morning meeting. Dave tried to talk but started to cry and couldn't continue. I took over and shared that his dog had died.

Several students hugged Dave, and many raised their hands to share their own losses. We listened to stories of turtles, dogs, cats, grandparents, and neighbors who had died. It was one of the most powerful teaching moments I've ever experienced. Together we laughed, cried, and realized that all of us had experienced or would at some point experience loss.

Consider reading your students *The Tenth Good Thing About Barney* (1971) by Judith Viorst or *When a Pet Dies* (1988) by Fred Rogers. After reading, students can list all the good things about any pets or loved ones they've lost. Obviously, this lesson needs to be handled with care.

5

Feelings and Emotions

Do you ever daydream about living a better life? Many of us
don't realize how our feelings and emotions affect almost
every aspect of our lives. That's why we need to slow down,
take stock, and become more attuned to how we feel.

Emotions originate as sensations in the body and are
always present, even when we are not aware of them.
Feelings are influenced by emotions but are generated by
mental thought patterns. Developing healthy emotional
awareness, first with ourselves and then in the classroom
with our students, helps improve relationships. And as
every teacher knows, teaching is all about relationships.

Take Stock of Your Inner Weather

In the depths of winter, I finally learned that within me there lay an invincible summer.

—Albert Camus

Does your inner state fluctuate like the wind? You've got good days, great days, lousy days, and days you don't ever want to remember. That's called life. Start tuning in to how you feel based on what you did yesterday. Can you identify any factors within your control that negatively affect your mood? You might notice some patterns.

Practice

I've found it helps to chart how happy I feel on a scale of 1 to 10. This accomplishes a few things: It's a nice reminder that when things aren't so good, this too will pass. It also helps us to notice what might be affecting our inner state. Sunday morning blahs? Maybe it was the alcohol and cheese plate the night before. Mean on Monday? Maybe the beginning of the work week is doing a number on your optimistic outlook. Exhausted on Friday? Maybe you haven't incorporated enough time in your work week for restoration. Simply assign a number to each day based on how you feel. You could even do it with your students, so they realize that teachers have bad days, too!

Student Connection

Set up a system where students can track how they feel every day on a scale of 1 to 10. Encourage them to do one thing a day to raise their happiness number. You can begin the day by asking students to record their numbers or simply hold up their fingers to share. Allow students to share why they chose that number and remind them that the numbers can change several times throughout the day. Just because the first two hours of the day were a 2 doesn't mean the rest of the day will remain that number. This exercise is teaching them (and reminding you) that everyone has some control over how they feel.

Feel It to Heal It

If we never let children go through the full wave of emotions when the emotion hits, there won't be the assurance that it will pass. That is scary.

—Krysten Taprell

Are you someone who feels things viscerally, or do you stuff your feelings down? Do you pay attention to that gut sensation that tells you something is off? If you pay attention to how you feel, you'll notice that your feelings affect the rhythm of the day. The best thing you can do is to notice, allow, and then let go. It's easier said than done, but worth the effort. Suppressed emotions fire up the nervous system even more than expressed unpleasant ones. Allowing yourself to feel emotional pain is a necessary step in rerouting your brain away from it. We can develop emotional capacity and learn to have greater comfort within the full range of our fluctuating emotions.

Practice

The next time you're feeling less than peaceful, allow the feeling to just be and ask what it might be trying to tell you. See if you can name the feeling. Redirect any tendency to overanalyze and perseverate on the negative feeling. Know that feelings come and go; no feeling is permanent. This too shall pass. Think back in your life to all the times you've had highs and lows; don't spend your energy worrying that the lows will be forever.

Student Connection

When students read a story or watch a movie in class, have them guess how the characters are feeling and explain their guesses. See if they can mimic the face that shows that feeling. This is the first step in teaching children to develop their inner "self-observer."

Have students form pairs and face their partner. One student pretends they are looking in the mirror and pantomimes an emotion while their partner acts like the reflection. See if they can then name the feeling they were pantomiming.

Consider showing students the 2015 film *Inside Out,* which explores how an 11-year-old girl named Riley learns to manage her conflicting emotions by mindfully embracing them.

Savor the Sunshine

O sunlight! The most precious gold to be found on Earth!

—Roman Payne

There is a reason behind the term "sunny disposition." Exposure to sunlight is thought to increase the brain's release of a hormone called serotonin, which is associated with boosting mood and helping a person feel calm and focused. Research (Mead, 2008) indicates that exposure to sunlight in the morning can help you sleep better at night. The sun is also the primary source of vitamin D, which strengthens the immune system. For these reasons, it's a good idea to get 15–30 minutes of morning sun every day.

Practice

Try to start and end your day by noticing and appreciating the sunrise and the sunset. Make every effort to spend at least 15 minutes outside appreciating the sun.

Student Connection

Consider taking your students outside to read in the warmer months or doing sidewalk-chalk math on the playground. Perhaps you could hold a morning meeting outdoors? There are many options for integrating sunshine into the school day.

Try the sunshine-shadow experiment. Take your students outside early in the morning and trace their shadows with sidewalk chalk. Have them predict what will happen to their shadows in the afternoon. Once afternoon arrives, go back outside and trace their shadows again. Compare the morning and afternoon tracings and discuss what may have caused their shadows to change. Have students stand in a line, holding hands, and snap a photo of their shadows. Then print the photo and have students label their shadows with their names. Repeat this activity in the same spot at the end of the year and notice any changes in the height of the children's shadows.

To encourage students to notice the power of light, place a prism in your classroom. Beautiful rainbow colors will bounce off it and catch their eyes throughout the day.

Write Yourself into Well-Being

I will write myself into well-being.

—Nancy Mair

The act of writing is a release—and often that's all we need to improve our mood. It's much like venting to a friend: We feel better after unburdening our souls.

Practice

Keep a journal where you record some of the practices in this book as well as your responses to them. You don't need to journal daily, but it can help to have all the notes, ideas, and practices you want to remember in one place.

Write about your feelings without placing any pressure on yourself or revising what you write, and keep writing until you've cleared your thoughts. Start writing and all the worries and thoughts that lie dormant, just waiting for a chance to show themselves, will find their way onto the page. Notice that although many of your thoughts reflect how you feel, they may not necessarily be based on the truth.

Student Connection

Let your students choose or even make their own journals. Encourage them to write as though they are talking to a friend. Have them record their thoughts, feelings, and emotions. Use this as an opportunity to teach them the difference between emotions and feelings. Pettinelli (2019) describes emotions as originating as sensations in the body, whereas feelings are influenced by our emotions but generated by our thoughts.

Mood Music

Where words leave off, music begins.

—Heinrich Heine

There is something about music that can immediately change your inner state. It's good to feel deeply, and music can be a conduit to getting in touch with your emotions.

Practice

Make your own mellow playlist. Or, if you prefer, create an uplifting mix. Better yet, both!

Student Connection

Introducing your students to various genres of music can be inspiring for both you and them. When children arrive at school, have music playing in the background. Having students enter the school with music piping through the halls sets a definite mood. You can also use music to calm students down or energize them.

Have students share their favorite songs with you. Consider playing their favorites while they are working quietly. If a favorite is an upbeat song, save it for an afternoon dance party before dismissal. Keep a request box available for students to submit their favorite songs. Many students enjoy listening to instrumental music as they work, as it can help them to focus.

Reframing Pessimism

You'll never find a rainbow if you're looking down.

—Charlie Chaplin

Pessimistic thinking involves consistent thought patterns about why bad things happen. A sense that "it's all my fault—I always mess up everything" is common. Because pessimistic people expect bad things to happen, bad things often *do* happen. Helplessness, low self-esteem, and chronic worry do nothing to uplift yourself or others.

Practice

Next time you find yourself having pessimistic thoughts, see if you can reframe them by finding the humor in the situation. When used in the right way, humor can positively shift your perspective. Laughing feels good and can interrupt negative thought patterns.

Student Connection

When your students are feeling pessimistic or just reflexively complaining, try the "One Complaint, but Life Is Great" activity. Have them all stand in a circle and share one complaint apiece. After each person shares, everyone yells out in unison, "But life is great!" You will be amazed by the amount of laughter this generates. It is also a nice lesson in compassion and common humanity.

Mental Health Days for Students

Each person deserves a day away in which no problems are confronted, no solutions searched for.

—Maya Angelou

Should students get mental health days? After all, school can be stressful. A report from the Centers for Disease Control and Prevention (Leeb et al., 2020) found that the proportion of mental health–related emergency department visits for children ages 5–11 and 12–17 increased by about 24 percent and 31 percent, respectively, between 2019 and 2020.

We need to make mental health a priority, not an afterthought. One step in this direction is to give students more autonomy to identify their needs. Setting clear parameters and boundaries is essential—we don't want students to use mental health as an excuse to avoid school—but allowing two mental health days a year sounds reasonable.

Practice

Model good mental health for students by treating your emotional well-being like you do your physical well-being. If you were to break your leg or wake up with the flu, you wouldn't go to work that day, and the same should be true of being depressed or anxious. Don't just power through—stop and take care of yourself. Try not to make this a habit, but it's OK to take a day to regroup, refresh, and restore.

Student Connection

Foster your students' mental health by allowing them to participate in technology-free activities of their choice for five minutes every day. To help students choose an activity that truly improves their mental health, come up with a list of options they can select from. Spend time exploring the benefits of the different activities with students.

Create a mental health activity box in your classroom. Begin with your own and then collect suggestions from students and colleagues. Once a week, have a student select one activity for the class to do. Here are some possible options:

- Mindful coloring
- Circling feelings on a feelings chart and discussing them
- Playing musical instruments or listening to music
- Playing charades
- Painting with watercolors

Let It Go

Dare to live by letting go.

—Tom Althouse

Stop resisting what is; simply let it be. If you can do that, you've eliminated 99 percent of your problems.

Practice

Can you let go of whatever resistance you're feeling in the present moment? Imagine if you decided to accept every single situation in your life as being in your best interest.

Inhale and say to yourself "let," then exhale and say "go."

Student Connection

Blow up balloons and ask your students to write messages using the sentence frame "I accept _____." Then attach the messages to the balloons and release them as you play the song "Let It Go" from the 2013 movie *Frozen*. If you can't or prefer not to use real balloons, have students draw balloons and write the things they want to let go of in each one. When they're done, guide them to imagine their balloons floating away, high into the sky.

Disagreeing Without Being Disagreeable

You can disagree without being disagreeable.

—Ruth Bader Ginsburg

Have you ever had to file a complaint or speak up about a negative experience? If so, were you angry or kind? What was the outcome? Our attitude often shapes reactions from others. If you're positive, people tend to react to you positively. When you have a negative attitude, you attract negativity.

When you have a disagreement with someone, share your convictions without judging the other. As teachers, we must frequently confront others and advocate for our students. When we do this in a kind but firm manner, we are communicating that we will always act on behalf of the students. You'll find you earn more respect with this attitude than by being either disagreeable or a pushover.

Practice

Consider a situation in your life where you need to stand up for yourself. Take the time to formulate your words so that they convey kindness, compassion, and, most important, respect.

Student Connection

Teaching students to engage in discourse without judgment may be one of the most valuable lessons we can impart. Our world is full of examples of those who turn people they disagree with into the enemy. There is another way. We can agree to disagree without judging or belittling.

Model listening to alternative viewpoints without interrupting or raising your voice. Taking in another's perspective develops our empathy and compassion.

Hold a weekly morning meeting where students are encouraged to discuss any suggestions for improving the classroom environment. Alternatively, they could write down their suggestions anonymously and place them in a suggestion box to be read aloud and discussed.

Emotional Contagion

Emotion goes inside-out. Emotional contagion, though, suggests that the opposite is true. If I can make you smile, I can make you happy. If I can make you frown, I can make you sad. Emotion in this sense goes outside-in.

—Malcolm Gladwell

Emotional contagion is a tacit exchange that can occur between people in under a second in certain situations. It occurs on many levels, including at the neural network level, and can be negative or positive. For example, if someone approaches us with a smile, we have a natural tendency to smile back. If they approach us with a frown, our tendency is also to frown. We're not always fully conscious of this tendency.

Yawning is another example of emotional contagion. It reflects our brain's inclination to synchronize with others through our mirror neurons, potentially boosting group cohesion and social bonding (Ferrari & Coudé, 2018).

Practice

Don't turn a blind eye to the effects your relationships have on you. Some people are positive forces who elevate your mood, while others drain you of optimism and serenity. When you become aware that you feel emotionally depleted when you're around a certain individual, limit your exposure to them.

Likewise, your emotions can have an impact on your students, so it's important to calibrate your emotional state before you enter your classroom each day. Remember: Your emotions affect the classroom climate.

Student Connection

Emotions influence how students learn. For example, a confident child will tend to feel more secure in the classroom, which may increase their ability to listen to information well, learn, and take risks. In contrast, an anxious or fearful child may be unable to pay attention and process that same information. Once again, the social-emotional aspect of teaching and learning and its impact on academic achievement is profound.

Grumpy for No Reason?

It is not a person or situation that affects your life; it is the meaning you give to that person or situation which influences your emotions and actions. Your choice is to change the meaning you gave it or to change your response, in order to create the outcome you want.

—Shannon L. Alder

Our brains are hardwired for picking up on the emotions of others—it's a bit like a telepathic ability. My daughter can tell from the way I say hello when I answer the phone what my state is. This is one of many reasons why it's so important to be aware of our emotions.

Mehrabian (1981) found that 7 percent of what we communicate is the result of the actual words we say; 38 percent is due to factors like tone of voice, timbre, tempo, and volume; and a whopping 55 percent is communicated nonverbally through things like our body posture, the way we breathe, and how we move.

Before we can even think about changing how we feel, we have to be tuned in to how we feel. Feeling grumpy? Ask yourself why you feel that way. What triggered the feeling? Remember that our moods can have a profound impact on the emotional states of others.

Practice

The people we are closest to often absorb or deflect our negativity. It's OK to feel negative emotions, but you have to own them and try not to spread them. You can start by acknowledging how you feel to others so they don't think they are the cause of your grumpiness. Sometimes this is enough to shift the intensity of the feeling.

Student Connection

As a class, read Jory John's 2022 book *The Sour Grape*, about a grudgeful grape who is grumpy toward his friends over lots of little things. After reading, discuss the power of forgiveness and getting over the little things. Discuss whether there are any benefits to holding a grudge and staying in a negative mood.

Wishing

You are never given a wish without also being given the power to make it come true.

—Author unknown

The things I wish for have changed over the years. I rarely wish for material success or greater achievement these days, more often wishing simply for peace of mind and heart. I want to wake up every day feeling content, optimistic, and confident that I can handle whatever comes my way. I want to feel still and relaxed inside. That's why I wrote this book. Each day is a path to possibly uncover and remember the peace we once had but have forgotten.

Practice

Get quiet and ask yourself not what you *want*, but how you want your heart and mind to *feel*. Even when we want a specific thing, it's the feeling of having it that we crave, not the thing itself. Next, think about what you could do to get this feeling and what it will be like when you have it. Write down your thoughts using vivid language. When you're done, wish for the support and guidance to lead the way. Finally, let go and trust you'll get what you're looking for.

Student Connection

Have your students write a word or phrase on a sticky note that captures how they would like to feel. Place the stickies in a designated spot in your classroom to create a wishing wall. Students may also write wishes for others. Use colored stickies for a great visual display that is easy to update throughout the year.

If You Can't Name It, Does It Exist?

Out of sight is out of mind.

—Arthur Hugh Clough

Some Indigenous languages have no word for the act of telling a lie—the concept is simply not a part of their languages because it isn't part of their thinking or behavior (Hemley, 2003). Without a word for the concept, it doesn't seem to exist. In fact, Hemley found that the Tasaday tribe in the Philippines reportedly has no words for *dislike, hate,* or *war*—what a thought!

Practice

Eliminate a negative word from your vocabulary. Once you are no longer using the word, see if it continues to show up in your behavior.

Student Connection

Have students write down any negative thoughts they are having and then cross them all out one at a time. This symbolizes getting rid of those thoughts forever! If time allows, have them write a positive thought to replace each negative one they've crossed out.

Be a Reservoir of Joy

Joy is prayer; joy is strength; joy is love; joy is a net of love by which you can catch souls.

—Mother Teresa

In *The Book of Joy,* the Dalai Lama and Archbishop Desmond Tutu (Dalai Lama et al., 2016) write that joy is connection: The more we turn toward others, the more joy we experience, and the more we can share our joy with them. The goal is not just to create joy for ourselves but, as the archbishop poetically phrases it, "to be a reservoir of joy, an oasis of peace, a pool of serenity that can ripple out to all those around us" (pp. 63–64). Every day is a new opportunity to begin again. We must begin each day understanding that joy is already present in us; it arises through simple moments of love, gratitude, and hope.

Practice

Who is the most joyful person you know? Write down their name. What makes them so joyful? Is it that they're particularly authentic, sincere, appreciative?

Search out what brings you joy or what used to bring you joy. Is there a dimmer switch on your inner light right now? If so, how can you make that light brighter? Is there a new recipe you could try and share with a neighbor or someone in need? Perhaps a poem or a letter you could write and send to a friend? Notice how spreading joy yields more joy for everyone.

Student Connection

To teach students that joy is contagious, begin by explaining what *contagious* means. Tell them that both good things, like laughter, and bad things, like sickness, can be contagious. Then, write the word *joy* on many different-colored stickers and pass them out so that each student has a "bunch of joy." Take students outside and tell them to chase one other around and "spread joy" by tagging their classmates with stickers. When the game is over, you can hold a whole-class discussion about how it made students feel, what joy means to them, and what activities and experiences in their own lives bring them joy.

Recognize and Release Stress

The greatest weapon against stress is our ability to choose one thought over another.

—William James

According to the physician Gabor Maté (2011), research has identified three factors that universally lead to stress: uncertainty, lack of information, and loss of control.

If aliens from another planet were to eavesdrop on humans, I wonder how many times they would hear the word *stress*. They'd probably wonder what it was, since you can't see it, you can't touch it, and you certainly can't contain it. So, can we release it? The answer is yes—at its core, stress is fear, and we can release fear.

Practice

When you feel stressed, follow the steps of the STOP process:

- **S**top.
- **T**ake a breath.
- **O**bserve the feeling of unwanted stress; acknowledge it; and thank it, for it only wants to protect you.
- **P**roceed.

Student Connection

Play the cooperative learning game Just Like Me, which helps students build connections with their peers. Read aloud a variety of statements about situations in which students may feel uncertain or worried. For example, you might say, "You sit down in class and realize there's a math test you totally forgot about" or "As you boarded the school bus, you remembered you left your homework and lunch on the kitchen counter." As you read each statement, everyone to whom it applies stands up, says, "Just like me," and sits down again.

Trust Your Emotions

Emotions make us human. Denying them makes us beasts.

—Victoria Klein

How do you judge your emotional experiences? Do you trust your emotions, or do you feel they are inaccurate? There is a reason we judge our emotions; it has to do with how our caregivers responded to them as young children. For example, I was told to keep my chin up, to stay busy, and not to wallow when I felt upset as a child. "We don't show our emotions, so keep them to yourself" was the message. Since then, I've had to retrain myself to allow myself not only to show my emotions, but to trust them as well.

Practice

If a friend told you they were upset about something, would you think their emotions were off, excessive, or wrong? Most likely not. The way we feel is the way we feel. The next time you notice an emotion, see if you are judging it or trying to avoid it. Do your best to validate and accept the emotion. See if you can make sense of why you would feel this way. Give yourself compassion. Not only is it OK to have emotions, it's what makes us human.

Student Connection

Encourage students to let their emotions out. You want to foster a safe space where students can name, feel, and trust their emotions. One way to talk about emotions is through role-play. Read students different scenarios that could warrant different emotions and have them act them out. For example: "You and your friends are playing a board game. All of a sudden, your dog runs through the living room and over your game. Game pieces go flying and you lose your spot on the board." Give this same prompt to a few groups of students and see what they come up with. Some students might think it is funny and not a big deal, while other students might be upset by the harm the dog causes. Invite students to share their emotions in a classroom discussion.

Fear Not

We should all start to live before we get too old. Fear is stupid. So are regrets.

—Marilyn Monroe

Fears are just thoughts—usually worries. They limit possibilities and hurt our minds and bodies. When we are afraid, we don't move forward but stay frozen in anticipation of what could happen. This is precisely the point at which we can reframe our fear by focusing on the best possible outcome rather than the worst-case scenario.

Practice

Write down what you fear. Is the fear based in truth, or does it stem from outdated or erroneous beliefs? Envision the worst-case scenario, then reframe and write down all the alternative positive outcomes that could occur instead. You are retraining your mind, creating new neural pathways that can change your negative, fearful thinking to positive and hopeful thinking.

Now get moving: Physical exercise boosts your energy and can make you feel stronger and more confident.

Student Connection

One of Fred Rogers's principles was "What is mentionable is manageable" (Kris, 2017). A related quote from Daniel Siegel and Tina Payne Bryson (2012) is "name it to tame it." Fears feel more manageable when they are named and acknowledged, and helping children to name overwhelming emotions has a taming effect, ensuring they feel heard, understood, and valued.

In your class, have students create characters that help to name emotions that will come up throughout the year. For example, you might create a character called "Freddy Fear" and talk with students about how to identify him and deal with him when he comes around.

Don't Resist Sadness

It doesn't hurt to feel sad from time to time.

—Willie Nelson

We tend to push away sadness, but sometimes it's by holding the feelings as fully as possible that a shift happens. Perhaps the feeling of sadness has a message. Maybe we have resisted a part of ourselves that wants to be heard.

Practice

The next time you feel sad, just allow the feeling. Don't cover it up, don't get busy, just feel the sadness and consider whether it has a message for you.

Listen to a soulful song as you compose a simple poem about how sadness feels in your body.

Student Connection

When students are sad, encourage them to write or draw how it feels. Put on some soulful music to mirror their mood. If they are making art, encourage them to express their feelings in colors. You can encourage them to use colored pencils and then go over the color with a bit of water as a way of "art journaling."

Where Are You Carrying Tension?

If you ask what is the single most important key to longevity, I would have to say it is avoiding worry, stress, and tension.

—George Burns

Often tension builds without our awareness, causing countless issues in the body. If we can train our minds to detect the tension in our bodies before it builds, we can release it before its grip takes hold. When the body is static for long periods, tension builds, so it's a good idea to move around as much as you can.

Practice

Progressive muscle relaxation (PMR) is an effective technique for reducing both bodily tension and psychological stress. This simple technique involves the alternate tensing and relaxing of the major muscles in your body from your head to your feet.

Start by tensing all the muscles in your face—make a tight grimace, close your eyes tightly. Hold this expression as you inhale slowly and count to 8. Then, exhale and relax completely. Let your face go completely lax, as though you were sleeping. Feel the tension seep from your facial muscles. Repeat the steps as you work your way down your body, with your neck, shoulders, and so on.

Student Connection

There are many opportunities to use PMR with students: during transitions, before an exam, and throughout the day to signal breaks. Here is a script you can use or modify:

> Get comfortable in your seat with your feet flat on the floor and arms unfolded. You can gently close your eyes or look down. Start by clenching your fists. Count to 10 slowly, then relax your hands. Feel the warmth and tingle. Stretch your fingers as though you are reaching piano keys that are far apart. Count to 7 slowly, then relax your fingers.
>
> Pull your shoulders up and try to have them touch your ears. Count to 7 slowly, then relax your shoulders. Now pull your shoulders back like a soldier, as far as you can. Count to 7 slowly, then relax.
>
> Imagine you are eating a lemon; scrunch up your face and hold it tight. Count to 7 slowly, then relax your face.
>
> Point your toes upward toward your knees and hold tight. Count to 7 slowly, then relax your toes.
>
> Take a cleansing breath and let any leftover tension drain out of your body.

Armor Up

A sense of humor… is needed armor. Joy in one's heart and some laughter on one's lips is a sign that the person down deep has a pretty good grasp of life.

—Hugh Sidey

Often, we are caught unaware when someone spews gratuitous criticism or insults at us. When this happens, we need a way to deflect their words so that we can protect our emotional state.

Practice

This practice helps to create a protective mental boundary. Next time you're the recipient of destructive comments, imagine you're wearing a suit of armor. When the negative words hit the armor, they bounce right off. It helps to have a good sense of humor and the ability to visualize. This strategy will help you internalize the process of deflecting harmful words instead of personalizing and accepting them as truth.

Student Connection

Talk with students about ways to deal with negativity or criticism. Should they rise above and ignore it? Should they confide in a teacher or another trusted adult? Perhaps they can use humor to ease the situation. Role-play how to respond to bullies, then pair students up and give them various scenarios, with one student acting as a bully and the other practicing a response. Bullies don't like to be ignored, so sometimes retreat is a better option than confrontation. Have students determine which strategy would work best for each scenario.

Sometimes an active grounding exercise can help us armor up against criticism. Have students stomp their left foot, then their right foot, and then exhale quickly but deeply. Instruct them to focus on the feeling of their feet on the floor as they continue the pattern of stomp, stomp, blow. Guide them to imagine that they are kicking out and blowing away their anxious thoughts.

Another grounding exercise to do with all students is to have them envision their body as a tree. Have them stand tall, sink their roots into the ground, and stretch their arms up into the sky just like a tree's limbs, swaying in the wind. Imagine the roots feeling the different energies of the Earth as they go deeper and deeper. This is a stance of power and confidence.

Heart Versus Head

Inner guidance is heard like soft music in the night by those who have learned to listen.

—Vernon Howard

As an academic, I'm surrounded by colleagues who live in their heads. I've found that an overreliance on either intellect or emotion—head or heart—can lead to an imbalanced outlook on life. I believe the best place to live is between the head and the heart, balancing logical thinking with visceral feeling.

Where do you live? Head, heart, or in between?

Practice

Think of a topic on which you need guidance. Write down a question about it, then listen for a response that comes from the heart rather than the head. As we learn to tune into the heart, our lives become more purposeful because our actions are aligned with our own inner knowing.

Student Connection

Teaching students to listen to their heart could alleviate countless sticky situations that young people get into. Help them to rely on their own intuition early on by asking them to connect with how it feels in their body when they do something wrong versus when they do something right. Have them identify where they feel this sensation. Most will say their heart or stomach. (Never have I had a student say that they feel it in their head.) Explain to them why it's important to make decisions with not just our brains but our hearts as well.

Riding Out the Storm

Remember, the storm is a good opportunity for the pine and the cypress to show their strength and their stability.

—Ho Chi Minh

When I'm inside, safe and dry, I love nothing more than a good storm. It's a vivid reminder that I'm not in charge. What I love even more is the morning after a storm: The air feels cleaner, the sun seems brighter, and the birds' songs seem cheerier. It always amazes me how resilient the trees, birds, plants, and animals are that weathered the storm.

So why, when we're faced with our own internal storms, do so many of us not trust that the morning after will come and all will be well again? This year, I've lost friends to suicide. I have no doubt they were battling internal storms they believed would never end. Sadly, I get it. When you are in the midst of pain of any kind, it's hard to be rational and nearly impossible to be hopeful. It's one of the few times the present moment is the worst place to be.

Practice

One way to help you prepare for unforeseen storms in your life is to make a list of all the storms you've weathered in the past—difficult times that came and went. It's a reminder of the law of impermanence—nothing lasts forever.

Student Connection

Have your student list their storms, then discuss how they were able to weather them. What made the experiences easier?

Lighten Up

Life is too important to be taken seriously.

—Oscar Wilde

The following story is taken from *The Art of Possibility* (2002) by Rosamund Stone Zander and Benjamin Zander:

> Two prime ministers are sitting in a room discussing affairs of state. Suddenly a man bursts in, apoplectic with fury, shouting and stamping and banging his fist on the desk. The resident prime minister admonishes him: "Peter," he says, "kindly remember Rule Number 6," whereupon Peter is instantly restored to complete calm, apologizes, and withdraws. The politicians return to their conversation, only to be interrupted yet again twenty minutes later by a hysterical woman gesticulating wildly, her hair flying. Again the intruder is greeted with the words: "Marie, please remember Rule Number 6." Complete calm descends once more, and she too withdraws with a bow and an apology. When the scene is repeated for the third time, the visiting prime minister addresses his colleague: "My dear friend, I've seen many things in my life, but never anything as remarkable as this. Would you be willing to share with me the secret of Rule Number 6?" "Very simple," replies the resident prime minister. "Rule Number 6 is 'Don't take yourself so g—damn seriously.'" "Ah," says his visitor, "that is a fine rule." After a moment of pondering, he inquires, "And what, may I ask, are the other rules?"
>
> "There aren't any." (p. 79)

Practice

Stop negativity in its tracks by refusing to take yourself—and life—so seriously. When things go wrong, go easy on yourself and others. Laugh more, stress less.

Student Connection

Humor in a classroom enhances students' interest and participation, and teaching students to laugh at themselves gives them a sense of control over those moments when they make mistakes. Have your students make a list of their worst moments and write about ways they might be funny now.

Tongue twisters are a great way to lighten the mood. You might also consider a quick game of charades or round of knock-knock jokes.

The Hedonic Treadmill

Psychologists sometimes refer to… the "hedonic treadmill": the idea that we're always working hard to change our life situation, but we actually never feel very different.

—Mark Manson

The *hedonic treadmill* is a metaphor coined by Brickman and Campbell (1971) for the human tendency to pursue one pleasure after another. It's based on the idea that people generally return to a level of happiness that's consistent with their personality and genetics. Essentially, we repeatedly return to our baseline level of happiness regardless of what happens to us.

The hedonic treadmill gives us the ability to continuously adapt to ever-changing situations. Happiness dissipates, anger calms, and sadness regresses. Despite extreme events and emotional fluctuations in daily life, emotional equilibrium is eventually regained.

Practice

When a negative event occurs, first acknowledge that it's normal to not feel OK, then identify at least two people you can share your feelings with. Remember, this too will pass. We tend to deal with situations better when we know they are temporary.

Student Connection

Have your students make a list of ways they can cope with difficult days. Make it clear that everyone feels bad sometimes. Have them brainstorm ways to cheer themselves up when they are feeling down. Talk about activities that are likely to cause lasting happiness, like learning a new hobby or connecting with friends. We want our students to realize that *things* don't contribute to happiness as much as people and meaningful activities do.

How Do You Feel?

When how you feel is more important than anything else, you'll start being careful of what you think.

—Author unknown

If asked, most of us would say we'd like to increase our store of positive emotions and discard the negative, not-so-helpful ones. That's understandable; emotional stress seems to deplete the body, whereas emotional calm revives it. The challenge is how to do this. Calm is something we need to seek out, whereas negative emotions and stress seem to find us easily.

Practice

One technique to calm your emotions is the Quick Coherence Technique from the HeartMath Institute (Childre et al., 2016). Follow these steps:

1. **Heart focus.** Focus your attention on the area around your heart. You can place your hand over the center of your chest if you like. If you notice your attention wandering, just shift it back to the area of your heart.
2. **Heart breathing.** Breathe deeply, but normally, and feel as if your breath is coming in and out through your heart area. Focusing on this area helps your mind stay focused and your respiration and heart rhythms synchronize. Breathe slowly and gently until your breathing feels smooth and balanced, not forced.
3. **Heart feeling.** As you maintain your heart focus and heart breathing, activate a positive feeling. Recall a time when you felt good inside and try to reexperience the feeling. For example, think of a special place you've been or the love you feel for a close friend or family member. Once you've found a positive feeling, you can sustain it by continuing your heart focus, heart breathing, and heart feeling.

Student Connection

When a student has strong negative feelings, work with them to reflect on why they feel this way. They might talk with you about it, complete a feelings reflection sheet, or draw a picture. Doing this helps students become more in tune with their emotions.

Play a feelings walking game while outside. Ring a chime and have everyone walk like they are angry. Ring the chime again and have the children walk like they are calm and confident. Repeat the activity with different emotions. Afterward, discuss how they felt when doing each one.

Mirror Neurons

When we are around people as well as images, we begin taking on their moods and emotions. Resonance is the driving force that makes this transference of energy and information happen. On a biological level, mirror neurons are part of the physical mechanism that causes us to emulate the images around us.

—Cary G. Weldy

Why do we cry during sad movies? Why do sports fans get so excited during a game? We are wired to mimic what we see. While observing, we can generate a brain state similar to that of the person or people we are observing because of the *mirror neuron system.*

Penagos-Corzo and colleagues (2022) suggest that mirror neurons are strongly associated with human empathy. Mirror neurons were first discovered in the 1990s, when neuroscientists found that when monkeys observed another monkey grabbing an object, the same neurons in their brains fired (Rizzolatti & Fabbri-Destro, 2010). These specialized neurons and their networks help explain how humans "mirror" one another, including our emotions.

Practice

Try an unofficial test of your mirror neuron system. See if you can perceive how someone feels without their saying anything. Or when you first walk into a meeting, see if you can "feel" the unspoken emotions before it begins.

Student Connection

The emotional environment of the classroom is affected by the way we group students. If you want an interactive group discussion, have students sit in a circle so they can all see one another. Notice if they begin to mirror one another in their responses and demeanor. Do you want to encourage independent, focused work? Have the students pick a spot to work where they are by themselves, facing a wall, and not close to others.

Negative Energy

Keep yourself away from negativity. Negative thinking depresses you. Negative people discourage you. Negative environment brings you down.... Positive thinking inspires you. Positive people encourage you. Positive environment pushes you up. Team up with positivity.

—Jacinta Colney

Some people are chronic negativity carriers, depots of pent-up anger and unpredictable emotions. Some remain trapped in victim mode at all times and act in ways that only further their victimization. Negative energy can have a powerful pull on us, especially if we're struggling to maintain positive energy and balance. It may seem that others who exude negative energy would like to pull us into the darkness with them. We do not have to go. Without passing judgment on them, we can decide that it's OK to walk away, OK to protect ourselves.

Practice

Set boundaries with those who pull you into negative thought patterns, such as chronic judgment, worry, and gossip. Realize it's not about you; it's about them. Assume the role of the unattached observer. You can even imagine yourself in an invisible bubble. If you can, disengage from the person or the situation.

Student Connection

Write a recipe for negativity with your students. For example:

Negativity
Ingredients:
2 angry eyes
1 frown
2 hunched shoulders
10 clenched fingers
1 loud voice
2 closed ears

Combined, all this makes for one very negative emotion. When you notice this in others, give them the space they need, but if you can, walk away and choose to either be by yourself or interact with someone else. Don't try to change the person with the negativity.

Next, have your students write a recipe for positivity. Brainstorm ingredients as a class but allow each student to customize their own recipe.

6

Kindness and Gratitude

The powerful combination of kindness and gratitude should not be underestimated. Kindness is a force of goodness, a loving presence that can bring comfort and solace to us and others. Gratitude is more than a simple expression of thanks; it's a way of being and experiencing the world, shifting our mindset from what we lack to what we have.

The kindness and gratitude practices in this chapter have a ripple effect in your teaching, especially when you use the student connections in your classroom. When you engage in the practices regularly, the ripple effect will expand to family, friends, colleagues, and even perfect strangers.

Photograph What Matters Most

We take photos as a return ticket to a moment otherwise gone.

—Katie Thurmes

Finding greater meaning in our lives can improve our perspectives and help us cope with stress. We can find meaning in the mundane, as well as in the special moments that we want never to forget. Taking time to capture and appreciate what matters most to us can help us focus on the positive. One way to do this is through photography.

Practice

Over the next week, take photos of things that make you smile or that matter to you. These could be photos of family, friends, pets, nature, or possibly even other photographs. Try to take at least one a day. Import these photos into a slideshow that you can use to introduce yourself to your students. Take the time to explain what each photograph represents and why it is meaningful to you.

Student Connection

Have students create their own visual representations of what matters most to them in, for example, a slideshow or collage format. Images give students who express themselves better visually than verbally an opportunity to share an important part of their lives or personalities.

Giving Gratitude

At times our own light goes out and is rekindled by a spark from another person. Each of us has cause to think with deep gratitude of those who have lighted the flame within us.

—Albert Schweitzer

Emmons (2016) states that gratitude has two key components. The first is recognizing that there is goodness in the world and that we have been the recipients of gifts—big and small—along the way. The second is understanding that the source of this goodness lies outside us. Yes, we have accomplished some things on our own, but if we look back, we can see that the path to our accomplishments is lined with others who have supported us.

Practice

How many people have had a hand in your success? Focus your attention on what other people have done for you in the past week. Have you shown them how grateful you are for their support? Gratitude is reciprocated when we thank others for their kind acts.

List times when you've acted in a way that was kind, patient, or generous toward someone. As you look at this list, how does it feel to own this part of you? Where in your body do you feel it? Remind yourself of this list every day for the next week.

Now take a moment to picture what your life would be like if you didn't have all the things you're grateful for. Very quickly you'll start to appreciate just how fortunate you really are!

Student Connection

Keep a gratitude jar in the classroom. When you are grateful for something, record it on a slip of paper and add it to the jar. No names are necessary. Encourage students to do the same. Read the gratitude slips weekly. Together, you'll begin to realize how much good there is in the world.

A variation on the gratitude jar is gratitude chains. Have students generate a list of those who have supported them, adding specifics if they wish. Next, they can choose one selection to write on a strip of paper and decorate. Link all the students' strips into a chain to display in the classroom or hallway. These chains can be added to throughout the year. This is a great way for students to become aware of all those who help them.

Good Days

If you don't think every day is a good day, just try missing one.

—Cavett Robert

Do you ever find yourself worrying right in the middle of an otherwise good day that the good feeling can't last? Have you ever ruined a perfectly good mood by assuming it was probably the "calm before the storm"? We have the power to reframe this mindset. Think of the lyrics to Pink's "All I Know So Far": "This life is ours to choose—darkness comes and goes / But you can live like your life is on the line."

Practice

Today, enjoy and savor what is good. Be present and aware of positive feelings without speculating about how long they will last.

Student Connection

As a class, read Judith Viorst's classic *Alexander and the Terrible, Horrible, No Good, Very Bad Day* (1972). Have students discuss whether some of the bad things that happened to Alexander could have been avoided. Then, have them write a sequel to the story—about the next day, when everything goes right. Explain that although there will always be bad days, every new day is a chance to course-correct and begin again.

The Ripple Effect

While it may seem small, the ripple effect of small things is extraordinary.

—Matt Bevin

Small changes that happen at a micro level have far greater implications than we can imagine. This is what's known as the ripple effect. Any positive changes you make to your life will affect not only you, but also your friends, family, colleagues, and students far into the future.

Practice

Start a ripple effect by letting someone know they've made a positive difference in your life. As teachers, we don't get enough recognition, so take a moment to recognize a fellow educator for the good work they've done.

Student Connection

Ask your students to identify someone who has made a difference in their life and encourage them to directly reach out to that person. Perhaps they could reach out to a different person each day using a different form of communication, like this:

- Monday: Send someone a text or an email.
- Tuesday: Record and send a voice memo.
- Wednesday: Write an old-fashioned letter or postcard and mail it via snail mail.
- Thursday: Look someone in the eye and verbally express how they've affected your life.
- Friday: Make something and leave it with a note.

Appreciating What Remains

The aim of life is appreciation; there is no sense in not appreciating things, and there is no sense in having more of them if you have less appreciation of them.

—Gilbert K. Chesterton

When my sister and I cleaned out my mom's home after she died, I once again vowed to have less stuff and to appreciate what I have. Less really is more. When we remove the surplus, we can more genuinely appreciate what remains. Rumor has it that when my great-grandfather was a young boy, he had only one book, *A Tale of Two Cities* by Charles Dickens (1859/2012). I imagine he cherished that book more than I have any of the hundreds of books I've owned.

Practice

Books are meant to be shared. My wish for my birthday is that my husband will build me a lending library next to our mailbox where I can put books I'd like to share with others. What do you have that you could donate or share? Identify where you have a surplus of something and donate to others in need.

Student Connection

Have your students donate or share the books they've read. Take five minutes to go through their book collections and help them pick. Or have students donate unused toys for a toy drive. Often students have a surplus of toys that they may have outgrown or never really used.

Savor the Good

The present moment is filled with joy and happiness. If you are attentive, you will see it.

—Thich Nhat Hanh

Psychologist Rick Hanson (2013) has a great way to describe our internal negativity bias: "Bad news sticks to our brains like Velcro, and good news slides right off our brains like Teflon." One way to reverse this is to spend at least 15 focused seconds savoring whatever you encounter that's good in your life.

Practice

Writing down good news (and then taking a peek through your notebook or Notes app later) can slow you down and provide the intentional time needed to absorb good news into your long-term memory. Try it for a week. Focus on what you did right.

Student Connection

Have students record their own small positive accomplishments throughout the week. At the end of the week, have each of them share one good thing. Make it the norm for students to congratulate themselves on accomplishments big and small.

Revisiting Gratitude

The deepest craving of human nature is the need to be appreciated.

—William James

An exercise we don't often make time for is to deliberately choose to notice all that is working in our lives—to think about what we have received and what we have given. Gratitude connects us; it makes us feel good and do good. Has there been a time when something good has happened to you because of another person's action? Living gratefully means recognizing the good in our lives and recalling those who have supported us.

Practice

Think of a person in your life whom you have never taken the time to formally thank. Compose a letter of gratitude to this person describing specifically why you are grateful, how they have positively influenced your life, and the effect it has had on you. If possible, hand-deliver the letter and read it aloud. The next best option is to post it in snail mail. If neither of these is a possibility, of course, email would also work. Most important is to take the time to make sure this person knows you appreciate them.

Student Connection

Ask your students to record themselves thanking someone who has positively affected their life in the past week. As a homework assignment, have them share the recording with their parents or caregivers and send it to the person they're thanking. There is something moving about hearing a voice that conveys sincere gratitude.

Spread Kindness

Kindness can become its own motive. We are made kind by being kind.

—Eric Hoffer

Kindness is good for you and for everyone else, too. In his 2017 book *The 5 Side Effects of Kindness*, David Hamilton offers compelling scientific research showing that simple acts of kindness boost your physical, mental, social, and spiritual well-being.

Practice

Send someone a two-sentence email using this template: "Good morning, _____. I just wanted to say I'm thinking of you, and hope you have the best day." As simple as that. A single positive email can make someone's day.

Consider calling someone who you know is alone and could use a friend. Be there for someone who needs to talk and simply listen. Do a chore or a favor for someone else. Offer to babysit or visit someone who needs a friend.

Student Connection

Have your students create a "Sprinkle Kindness Like Confetti" bulletin board in the main lobby of your school. Encourage them to place a sticky note on the board with the name of someone who was kind to them that day. Students could even write a blurb describing the kind action. See how quickly your bulletin board can be covered with kindness!

You could also have students make a sign thanking someone who was kind to them to take to a local hospital, nursing home, or gym.

Anonymous Acts of Kindness

Don't judge each day by the harvest you reap, but by the seeds that you plant.

—Robert Louis Stevenson

Research (Luks & Payne, 2001) shows that helping others can be good for our mental health. Random acts of kindness inspire others to do the same. We often think we must do huge things to make a difference, when in fact it's the small things that can have the greatest impact. Rather than wait for a service opportunity, simply be open to what the present moment provides.

Practice

Extend some kind of unexpected generosity to various people for a week. Commit to one small random act of kindness each day. Extend your generosity to someone who least expects it. Consider anonymously sending a care package to someone, putting a treat on a colleague's desk, paying for a stranger's coffee, having flowers delivered to someone, providing doughnuts for the cafeteria workers, surprising the bus driver with a thank-you note and a pack of Lifesavers—the list of possibilities is endless.

Student Connection

Consider implementing a "Random Acts of Kindness Week" in your classroom or school during which students extend kindness to others. This could include thank-you cards, kindness sticky notes, or even a food drive. It's great for students to see what a difference kindness can make.

Discuss or have your students journal and reflect on how they feel after committing unsolicited acts of kindness.

Right Speech

Before you speak, ask yourself if what you are going to say is true, is kind, is necessary, is helpful. If the answer is no, maybe what you are about to say should be left unsaid.

—Bernard Meltzer

The world would be a quiet place if we only spoke what is true and kind. The Buddha teaches "right speech," meaning that we should abstain from four kinds of speech: false speech, slanderous speech, harsh or hateful speech, and idle chatter.

Practice

Today, notice whether the words you read in the media or hear in the course of conversation are true or kind. Do the words uplift you? Or do they make you feel low?

Commit to being kind today: Use kind speech; don't gossip; be an uplifter. Enter the faculty lounge with the intent to only contribute honest and kind words to any conversation.

Student Connection

Many young people today have grown up in a culture that publicizes things that used to be private—meals, outfit try-ons, daily routines, relationships—which opens them up to increased scrutiny. Take a tour of a social media site with your students and discuss the comments that are posted. Teach students the importance of communicating with kindness. Remind them that everyone is always helping us—either by being kind or by acting unkind and giving us the opportunity to choose kindness in response.

How Can I Help?

We don't have to do anything; sometimes the answer is in the thoughts we think.

—Author unknown

You've heard the saying "It's better to give than receive." This is backed up by research: When we help others, physiological changes occur in the brain that are linked with happiness (Kabat-Zinn, 2018). Helping others can make you feel rewarded and fulfilled and instill a sense of purpose. Sometimes just letting someone know you are willing to help is enough. I have friends who have texted me when I'm in need of support, and just knowing they are thinking of me helps.

Practice

If you're not sure what to do to support someone who is stressed or troubled, you can simply think of them and offer words of peace. Close your eyes and think or quietly say, "I offer you peace of mind" or "I offer you quietness."

Student Connection

Model ways to help others. For example, on the first day of school, you could introduce the custodian to the class, thank them for all they do, and ask how your class could support them to keep the school clean. You might do the same for bus drivers and cafeteria workers.

Toxic Positivity

Some days I'm not OK, and I'm not trying to fix that. No, I don't need advice on how to not feel this way. I just need time to feel it.

—Allyson Dinneen

I partially blame the happy-face emoji for the proliferation of fake happiness these days. Personally, I identify as neither an optimist nor a pessimist, but as a realist. The idea that we should have a positive mindset no matter what happens is neither practical nor healthy. No one should be expected to be constantly positive. Suppressing our true emotions can lead to stress, burnout, and shame.

Practice

Have you ever shared a difficult situation with a friend and received breezy advice in response that only made you feel worse? When someone shares that they are having a difficult time, refrain from offering advice and instead show empathy. Acknowledge that the best way to navigate negative emotions is to express, release, and process them. The best support we can give others is to validate their feelings and affirm that they have the ability to get through the situation.

Student Connection

If you've had a tough day, share this with students while emphasizing that you were able to get through it. Help them recognize that difficult times are a part of life. Discuss how we've all had difficult times.

Implement an empathy scavenger hunt. First, create a checklist of common negative situations for students: missing the bus, spilling cereal, forgetting homework, not getting picked for the team, and so on. Then have students circulate around the room and find a classmate who has experienced one of the situations until everything on the list has been checked off. If time allows, encourage students to respond to each person with empathy (not advice) about the situation they experienced.

Loving Kindness

Being deeply loved by someone gives you strength, while loving someone deeply gives you courage.

—Laozi

In her 1995 book *Loving-Kindness,* meditation teacher Sharon Salzberg describes "loving-kindness" as a compassionate practice to connect, inspire, and motivate people to transform our world. Specifically, loving-kindness meditation "is a practice and technique in which the central object we rest our attention on is the silent repetition of certain phrases ... a way of offering, gift-giving, and switching our attention" (Mindful.org, n.d., para. 9). In a landmark study, researcher Barbara Fredrickson and colleagues (2008) found that practicing seven weeks of loving-kindness meditation increased love, joy, contentment, gratitude, pride, hope, interest, amusement, and awe.

Practice

Practice loving-kindness meditation by silently repeating phrases offering kindness to yourself, those whom you love, those you may not know well, and perhaps those with whom you are having a difficult time. You may start by saying, "May I be safe. May I be happy. May I be healthy. May I live with ease." Customize these phrases to make them work for you. Then extend these phrases to the other people you've chosen to focus on. I find that if I repeat a loving-kindness mantra to myself during meetings when I'm feeling less than loving toward a colleague, it can shift the energy.

Student Connection

Brainstorm with students what kindness is. What are some acts of kindness they've experienced? What are some ways you can be kind to one another in the classroom? Discuss whether it's possible to be kind to someone we don't know or who isn't kind to us. Help them select a phrase they could use to send kind thoughts to themselves.

Share this mantra with students: "May I be happy. May I be kind. May I live in peace." Have students repeat the words silently to themselves. Next, have them think of someone they love and send the same phrases of kindness to that person. Then ask them to practice "stealth kindness," where they send the same kind thoughts to someone they do not know personally, such as a person they passed on the street. Finally, have them envision someone they are having a tough time with. Ask students whether they can send kind thoughts to someone whose actions they don't love.

1

Mind Management

Many of us experience common errors in thinking known as *cognitive distortions*. These distortions are patterns of thought that can negatively affect how we perceive reality, experience emotions, and behave. Through the practices in this chapter, you'll learn how to recognize and master your thoughts. You and your students will discover that these distortions are a normal part of being human and often show up when we're stressed or overwhelmed. You'll practice identifying, challenging, and reframing your unhealthy thinking patterns. With time and practice, your mindset will increase your emotional resilience.

The impact of our thoughts cannot be overestimated. When we manage our minds, we transform our lives.

Mental Time Travel

Every thought we think is creating our future.

—Louise Hay

Anyone who has ever tried to sit silently in a room and quiet their thoughts will agree that we have undisciplined minds. Our thoughts ping-pong back and forth. To rein them in, we have to first be aware of how unruly and disruptive they can be. Then we need to question them.

Practice

Try to sit without doing anything for one minute. Where did your mind go in that minute? Was it present, or did it take you forward to the day ahead, or maybe back to the past? Dwelling on the past can dredge up unresolved emotions and trigger feelings of depression; worrying about the future can tip us into anxiety. With practice, we can learn how to gather and settle our scattered minds so that we don't engage in so much mental time travel and can experience the calm and peace that await below the turmoil of our overthinking.

Student Connection

Help students understand just how long a minute is. Set a timer and have them put their heads down until they think a minute has passed. You'll be amazed at their lack of time perception. Then, have them estimate how many thoughts they think they have in a minute, set the timer again, and have them tally how many thoughts they actually have. If it feels appropriate, lead them through the practice you did.

Truth Telling

There's room for all the people. There's room for all the ideas, all the stories. There's room for all the books. You speak your truth.

—Jennie Nash

Why do we lie? Often it is to avoid suffering painful consequences, shame, embarrassment, or conflict. Avoiding punishment is the primary motivator for both children and adults. We also lie to keep up an image. Sometimes we lie to spare the feelings of others.

Practice

What if you were to promise to never lie again? You'd be known for your brutal honesty, and people who were interested in the truth would value you. Sounds like a way to have a more authentic relationship. Those who said they wanted the truth but who were in fact more interested in praise would learn not to seek you out for your opinion.

Student Connection

Play Two Truths and a Lie with your class. Have students sit in a circle. One student shares three statements about themselves with the rest of the group. Two of the statements are true, and one is a lie. Everyone then guesses which statement they think was the lie. Once everyone has made their guess, the student reveals which statement was the lie.

Discuss with your class how you sense when a student is lying. For example, you can explain that you watch for changes in tone, rate of speech, and voice, along with nervous body language, all of which could be signs that the person is lying. Learning to detect when someone is lying involves paying attention to subtle expressions, often called *micro expressions*.

These activities can open a class discussion about people's motivations for lying and whether it's ever OK to lie.

Fear of Forgetting

Forgetting is like lighting a candle. The candle might disappear, but the wax is always there.

—Author unknown

The older I get, the weaker my short-term memory seems, which can be frightening (especially since my mother was diagnosed with Alzheimer's). Slow cognitive decline is to be expected as we age. Don't add fear of a disease to your worries, as this only increases stress and anxiety, both of which make us more forgetful.

One of the reasons we don't remember things is that we don't pay attention when they occur. Our divided attention negatively affects our memories.

Practice

Get enough sleep, exercise, and hydration. Play brain games like Lumosity, and practice remembering a mantra every day. Most important, notice when your attention is hijacked and consciously bring it back to the present moment. Commit to training your brain just as you would your body.

Student Connection

Talk with your students about any strategies they use to remember things. One strategy that deepens long-term memory *and* learning is *interleaving,* which means "interspersing multiple (but related) concepts to encourage connections between ideas or skills" instead of teaching content in discrete chunks (Ferlazzo, 2021).

Engaging in frequent formative assessment and using writing as a strategy to deepen content understanding are also practices proven to support retention and memory (Collins, 2022).

Open Up to Hope

A rainbow is a prism that sends shards of multicolored light in various directions. It lifts our spirits and makes us think of what is possible. Hope is the same—a personal rainbow of the mind.

—Charles Snyder

Happy people are hopeful. When you keep your sense of hope, you are open to possibilities. The more you nurture hope, the more optimistic you feel, which allows you to see things you may have overlooked. Hope is like following the breadcrumbs out of the dark woods, eyes on a bright light ahead. You aren't yet feeling the warmth of the light, but you have trust that you're on the right path.

Practice

Hope is always there; you simply have to be open to the possibility. What can you adopt a more hopeful stance about? Are there words or gestures of hope you can offer to someone having a difficult time? How can you inspire hope in someone else?

Student Connection

Model your optimistic thought processes out loud so students can see how you go from doom-and-gloom thinking to hopeful thinking. Demonstrate how to catch and shift negative thought patterns by changing your perceptions or your beliefs to help "unstick" yourself in an unhelpful, pessimistic place.

At a few points throughout the year, have students write "I hope" statements. At the beginning of the year, you can ask them to write their hopes and dreams for the new school year. Discuss how putting these hopes on paper can help you to manifest them. Collect the written statements for students to reflect on later in the year. Then, a few months into the school year, have students write new "I hope" statements and compare them with their original statements. Did any of their hopes come true? Have their hopes changed since a few months ago?

You Are Enough

Believing in our hearts that who we are is enough is the key to a more satisfying and balanced life.

—Ellen Sue Stern

Imagine if an advertisement said you were absolutely wonderful just the way you are. You look good, people want to be around you, and you have everything you need. There would be nothing to buy—which is why you'll never see such an advertisement.

Practice

Just for today, in this moment, accept yourself exactly as you are. Remind yourself that you are enough. You don't need to do or accomplish anything or prove yourself to anyone. Just be you. Notice how this makes you feel.

Student Connection

Have your students begin each morning by writing the heading "You are enough" in a journal and whispering the words aloud. Each day for the next week, students can write something they like about themselves under the heading. If time allows, they can share what they write with partners during morning meeting. As an extension activity, have them create a class mural with illustrations and captions portraying the many ways they are "enough."

Is It True?

An unquestioned mind is *the world of suffering.*

—Byron Katie

Many of our deepest beliefs are based on our own misunderstood perceptions. When we turn our judgments around and question our thoughts and beliefs, we start to realize that our perceived problems are often just stories we tell ourselves. All the events of our lives are opportunities to learn. To better understand this concept, I recommend reading Byron Katie's *Loving What Is: Four Questions That Can Change Your Life* (2003). In my trainings, I often have participants respond to the following four questions based on Katie's:

1. Are your negative thoughts true?
2. Can you be absolutely sure that they're true?
3. How do you feel when you think these thoughts?
4. Where would you be without these thoughts?

Katie's simple message has always helped me turn my negative thoughts around.

Practice

Today, notice every negative thought you have and ask yourself if it is absolutely, positively true. If not, let it go and find a better thought.

Student Connection

All children can benefit from learning Byron Katie's practice. Model the four questions for students when they express negative thoughts. For example, if a student says, "No one at school likes me," ask them if they know for sure that the statement is absolutely true. Katie and Wilhelm (2016) created a modern retelling of the classic folk tale "The Sky Is Falling," reimagined through the lens of Katie's four questions.

Worry Less

I've had a lot of worries in my life, most of which never happened.

—Author unknown

Want more peace? Worry less.

Why do people worry? Often, it's a first reaction to a perceived conflict, problem, or internal fear. Many feel that worrying shows you care. I think we superstitiously convince ourselves that a positive outcome is more feasible if we dwell on the problem. In fact, the opposite can be true: very often, worry blocks solutions. I once heard someone say that worrying is like praying for the worst outcome. It gives power to the problem rather than the solution.

Practice

When you feel worry, repeat the following mantra: "I can choose peace instead of this." Peace is a tool to cultivate and one of the best antidotes to worry. Solutions are more likely to arise naturally out of a peaceful state.

Another practice is to distract yourself from worry by counting backward from 100. Just as distracting a child can alleviate a tantrum, so too can our worries be dispelled by focusing on something else.

Move: Walk around the block, run in place, jump up and down, put on some exhilarating music and dance. Not only does this help distract you from worry, but it also gets the stagnant energy out of your system.

Student Connection

When students share that they are worried, it's important to validate their feelings while also expressing confidence that things will be all right. Have them practice the "3 Cs" approach:

1. **Catch it.** Each time a worry creeps in, write a brief description of it.
2. **Challenge it.** Challenge the worry. Is it warranted? Does it help the situation?
3. **Change it.** Replace the worry with what is actually happening in the present moment. Most worries are about the future; the present moment is just fine—and very often what we worry about never ends up happening.

When students have gone through this process a few times, they should have evidence that many of their worries never materialize, which can show them that it's OK to release their worry and think more optimistically. To reinforce the point, Kevin Henkes' 2010 classic *Wemberly Worried* makes for a great read-aloud.

A Place for Worries

If it's out of your hands, it deserves freedom from your mind, too.

—Ivan Nuru

Excessive worry can cause physical symptoms such as stomach, head, and back aches. Think about the word *ache* for a moment: It can mean "a longing for something." When you worry, you are longing to control a future problem rather than existing in the present moment.

Practice

Worrying is an expression of fear, but the focus of our worry is rarely what we are actually afraid of. Explore the roots of your worry through journaling. After you write about your worry, reread your entry and see if you can consider the problem from a different perspective. Even if the worst-case scenarios we dream up come to pass, they are rarely as devastating as we make them out to be.

Start a journal just for worries. Write anything that crosses your mind. Come back to this journal in a month and highlight any worries that came true.

Student Connection

Have students log and review their worries for a week. Can you help them see that most of the things we worry about never come to fruition? You could even designate a daily "worry period" to discuss their worries.

If you notice that students are anxious, have them follow the steps of the pursed-lip breathing technique:

1. Inhale through your nose with your mouth closed while slowly counting to two in your head.
2. Purse or pucker your lips as though you're about to whistle.
3. Exhale through your pursed lips while slowly counting to four in your head.
4. Repeat for several minutes, always exhaling for longer than you inhale.

I used to encourage students to whistle or chew gum when taking tests. Both strategies seemed to calm students down a bit.

Respond Differently

We cannot force others to behave differently if they disagree with us. But if we change what we are saying or doing, they may respond differently.

—Nabil N. Jamal

Once you know what triggers you and what your typical response patterns are, resolve to pay attention to them, recognize them, and respond in different ways.

Practice

The next time someone does something that triggers you, try to imagine them as a small child without a positive role model. Try to have empathy toward them before responding.

Student Connection

Our facial expressions reveal six fundamental emotions: happiness, surprise, fear, sadness, anger, and disgust. Teach your students to take the time to notice the faces and expressions of those they encounter. Guide them to be open and aware of the range of expressions they encounter on a typical day. Challenge them to respond with kindness when they meet someone who's displaying a negative emotion. Have them notice if the person's facial expression changes when they are treated kindly.

Only Good Things Today

Every day is a good day. There is something to learn, care, and celebrate.

—Amit Ray

Affirmation: *Only good things are coming my way.* Can you imagine if we began every day believing that no matter what happens to us, we will learn, grow, and make the best of it? We just need to work on our mindset; many of us have undisciplined thinking. Be intentional, affirm what you want, and use your mind in a positive way.

Practice

Upon waking tomorrow, let your first thought be "Thank you for another day."

Spend the day only putting healthy foods into your body.

Wear the clothes that make you feel the most comfortable.

Read something that inspires you and puts you in a positive frame of mind.

Surround yourself as much as possible with positive people.

Student Connection

Put notes in your students' desks with the following mantra: "Only good thoughts today." Have students write positive mantra notes to give out to their classmates or other students in the school. They might even post the notes in high-traffic areas on campus.

Turn Down the Chatter

You are not your mind.

—Eckhart Tolle

I know I'm not the only one who has voices in my head, constantly providing unsolicited feedback on everything I do. I also tend to revisit situations in my head and pretend I had responded differently. One recent night, I replayed one of the meetings I had been in earlier that day, only this time saying just the right thing at the most opportune moment. Sound familiar?

Practice

In her 1995 book *Bird by Bird*, Anne Lamott shares the following advice she received from a hypnotist for turning down the distracting chatter in her mind:

> Close your eyes and get quiet for a minute, until the chatter starts up. Then isolate one of the voices and imagine the person speaking as a mouse. Pick it up by the tail and drop it into a mason jar. Then isolate another voice, pick it up by the tail, drop it in the jar. And so on. Drop in any high-maintenance parental units, drop in any contractors, lawyers, colleagues, children, anyone who is whining in your head. Then put the lid on and watch all these mouse people clawing at the glass, jabbering away, trying to make you feel like shit because you won't do what they want—won't give them more money, won't be more successful, won't see them more often. Then imagine that there is a volume-control button on the bottle. Turn it all the way up for a minute, and listen to the stream of angry, neglected, guilt-mongering voices. Then turn it all the way down and watch the frantic mice lunge at the glass, trying to get to you. (p. 25)

I'm not quite sure why I find this hysterical, but I do—and more important, it works.

Student Connection

Have students try the 5-4-3-2-1 exercise to quiet their minds:

1. Scan your environment and describe *five* things you see.
2. Describe *four* things you hear. As you listen to the sounds, really focus your attention on the noise they make and fully experience them.
3. Describe *three* things you feel.
4. Describe *two* things you smell.
5. Say *one* thing you like about yourself.

By the time students have finished, their focus will be on the present moment, not on their mental chatter.

Everything Is Always Working Out

The only thing that we can know is that we know nothing, and that is the highest flight of human wisdom.

—Leo Tolstoy

We have been given the exact circumstances we require to develop our unique gifts. What a wonderful way to view difficulties. Often the very thing we think of as a disaster is precisely what we need to grow: That job you lost was perfect timing because it allowed something better to emerge. The boy who broke your heart would have ended up breaking your spirit. The friend who betrayed you taught you forgiveness.

The lesson in all this? Let go of your plan and trust that everything is always working out for you. You're in the right place at the right time. Trust the present.*

Practice

Take a moment and reflect on some of the most difficult events in your life and see if you can identify whether those events actually helped you grow.

When difficulties arise, repeat this mantra: "I am always in the right place at the right time. All is well."

Student Connection

Share the following scenario with your class: *Lucy's best friend Chloe is moving far away. She feels incredibly sad to be losing her best friend.* Then discuss with students how this negative event could turn into a positive one for both Lucy and Chloe. Finally, have students reflect and journal on a difficult personal experience that ended up helping them grow.

---

*I want to note that I in no way intend to minimize scary, shocking, or dangerous situations where "letting go" would certainly not apply. Those who have experienced a traumatic event may have symptoms that would warrant seeking professional help.

What Motivates You?

You can't be that kid standing at the top of the waterslide, overthinking it. You have to go down the chute.

—Tina Fey

The key to motivation is noticing what actually propels us into action. Life is full of things we don't want to do but must do anyway. How do we get those tasks done? Each one of us has a strategy that gets us through the daily grind. It's often as simple as just getting started and then taking one small step at a time.

Practice

If you're struggling to get motivated, try to make whatever you're doing more enjoyable, such as by listening to music while you do it. Another strategy is to break tasks into smaller, more manageable pieces; accomplishing one step will fuel your motivation for the next. Challenge yourself to see how much you can get done in 15 minutes. You can also promise yourself a reward for completing a task.

Student Connection

Play background music as students work and teach students how to chunk projects. Use a timer in the classroom and reward students for achieving their short-term goals.

On Mondays, have students vote on a free-time activity to do on Friday if they complete their weekly tasks. Taking the time to determine what motivates our students is time well spent.

The Power of the Mind

You should always be aware that your head creates your world.

—Ken Keyes Jr.

When we wake up naturally, slowly noticing the quiet around us, we allow our minds and bodies to transition gradually from sleep to waking life. The opposite of this is waking up to an alarm clock. The word *alarm* should alert us that this can't be a good way to begin the day.

I've never used an alarm. I count my internal clock as one of the gifts I was graced with. Before I go to bed, I just decide what time I'd like to wake up, and I always awaken at that exact time. This simple exercise demonstrates the power of our minds.

Practice

One informal practice that utilizes visualization is attempting to set an internal clock. One weekend evening, before you go to bed, decide what time you would like to awaken the next morning. Visualize that time on your clock. See how close you get to that exact time.

Student Connection

We can help our students recognize the power of their minds by teaching them about visualization. Tell your students that Michael Phelps, the most decorated Olympian in the world, used visualization every night from the age of 12 to see himself swimming the perfect race. Many athletes use visualization as a tool for improving performance and developing plans to achieve their goals (Stephen et al., 2022).

Ask students to think of something concrete they'd like to achieve, such as winning an upcoming race or doing well on a test. Then prompt them to relax, close their eyes, and slow down their breathing. Next, guide them to see themselves achieving this goal. Have them use all their senses and create a movie in their mind. Instruct them to practice this visualization for a week and then check back to see if anyone had success in visualizing and achieving their goals. Discuss what else they had to do to be successful.

Split Energy

I learned a long time ago that there is something worse than missing the goal, and that's not pulling the trigger.

—Mia Hamm

Few things feel worse than indecisiveness. This is a kind of split energy—you're unsure of what choice to make or which direction to go in. One part of you wants something, but the other part is afraid to go after what you want because you may fail or be seen failing.

Practice

Outline what it is you want. Next, list all the reasons you might *not* want to achieve it. If you look closely at your list, you might notice that fear is behind many of your reasons. Decide whether your fears are warranted and if what you want is worth the risk. Often, you'll find that by identifying the root cause of your indecisiveness, you can choose a clear direction with more confidence.

Student Connection

When a student can't make a decision, tell them to flip a coin: Heads means *X*, tails means *Y*. If the coin landed one way and they are disappointed, then they know to make the opposite decision. Either way, they have clarity.

Mental Tennis

Never cut a tree down in the wintertime. Never make a negative decision in the low time. Never make your most important decisions when you are in your worst moods. Wait. Be patient. The storm will pass. The spring will come.

—Robert Schuller

How many decisions do elementary teachers make in a day? Borko and Shavelson (1990) are often cited as saying that teachers make *more than 1,500* decisions each day. And that's old research—I imagine the number has escalated since then. No wonder we get weary. Decision making can be a kind of mental tennis, with our minds going back and forth endlessly on what to do. Even the smallest decisions can sometimes feel overwhelming. When this happens, you need to stop and give your mind something else to do. When you come back to considering the decision later, you'll be in a more resourced state and have more clarity.

Practice

Although some decisions are no-brainers, many of the important decisions we face in life are complex, with no obvious solution. Hammond and colleagues (2015) explain that the need to make a difficult decision can cause anxiety, doubt, and confusion. They suggest that when you find you are playing mental tennis, you should "divide and conquer" by breaking your decisions down into the most relevant key elements: Focus on what's important, only collect as much information as necessary, and don't overanalyze. Personally, I create a pros and cons chart anytime I notice I'm playing mental tennis.

Student Connection

You can teach, practice, and model decision making in your classroom. Walk students through decisions like where to go on a field trip or what to do during choice time in the classroom; deciding between just two choices is best. Share the following steps with students for making sound decisions:

1. Identify the problem/conflict to be solved.
2. Gather relevant information.
3. Brainstorm possible solutions.
4. Identify potential consequences.
5. Make a choice.
6. Take action.

Always Believe That Something Wonderful Is About to Happen

Synchronicity is an ever-present reality for those who have eyes to see.

—Carl Jung

My daughter and I frequently repeat this mantra: "Things are always working out for us." And the truth is, when we remember to not only say this but also believe it, wonderful things do seem to happen. Synchronicities are abundant, so why not focus on the idea that something wonderful is about to happen?

Practice

Don't settle: If you desire something more than what you've got, it's OK to take steps toward achieving it. The right people will show up at the right time to support you. Events will occur that you couldn't have expected.

Student Connection

Talk to your students about the difference between synchronicity and coincidence. Whereas a coincidence is just an unexpected convergence of events with no particular significance, synchronicity is like a personalized message—a *meaningful* coincidence. Many would say that the study of synchronicity is pseudoscience; synchronistic events occur randomly, and it's thus far scientifically impossible to test whether they are connected in some meaningful way. Personally, I tend to believe that there are few coincidences and many synchronicities. The truth is that no one really knows for sure.

Encourage students to notice and log synchronicities in their lives for a week. They are training their brains to look for things in life that work out, which can counteract negativity bias—the tendency to weigh negative information more heavily than positive (Kiken & Shook, 2011). Having students notice and celebrate what goes right can help them view life as a series of opportunities and possibilities.

In Our Dreams

The future belongs to those who believe in the beauty of their dreams.

—Eleanor Roosevelt

Dreams can be a means of learning about ourselves. We know that during dreams we are consolidating our memories. Many Indigenous tribes consider dreams an important source of wisdom. Many find that dreams can lead to creativity and problem solving.

Practice

When you go to sleep tonight, ask yourself to dream. This does not guarantee that you will dream, but setting the intention right before you drift off to sleep gives your subconscious mind something to ponder. Place a dream journal next to your bed, and if you do dream, record what you recall as soon as you wake up.

Student Connection

Foulkes (1999) found that for the first two to three years of life, young children are mostly dreamless. They don't possess the language or abstract thought needed to process dreams. Dreams begin to accompany REM sleep at around 3 to 4 years old. Between the ages of 5 and 9, children begin to see moving images, characters in action, and multiple events strung together in their dreams. Children at this age also start to develop a greater ability to remember their dreams.

Take the time to discuss and normalize the process of dreaming with students. If students want to share details about their dreams, try to listen. If you can't listen, give them a piece of paper and crayons and have them draw what they remember. Even if they end up embellishing or making things up, they are still tapping into their imagination and expressing what's in their subconscious.

Monkey Mind

We're sitting under the tree of our thinking minds wondering why we're not getting any sunshine.

—Baba Ram Dass

Have you ever noticed the monkey in your mind? It's rarely still; it's either swinging toward the future or pivoting to the past.

We have about 60,000 thoughts a day. More than half of those thoughts are the same ones we had yesterday (Wilde, 2013). Hard to believe, but true. That's just what the mind does—think. However, with mindful awareness we can learn not to follow every single thought and let some of them simply dissolve. The first step is to be aware of how frenzied our minds can be.

Practice

Take an upright balanced seated position with good posture. Take one inhalation and exhalation, giving all your attention to your breath. Do this four times, counting after each respective exhalation. See what it feels like to pay attention to a single breath at a time. If you find your attention wanders, that's OK; just redirect it back to your breath.

Student Connection

Model the following breathing exercises for students, then add them to a "choice board" from which they can pick whichever one they like best. Students can sit or lie down for any of these.

- **Five-finger breathing.** Hold one hand out. With your other hand, trace up each finger as you inhale and then down as you exhale for five deep breaths.
- **Four-square breathing.** Slowly exhale all the air out of your lungs. Then, gently inhale through your nose to a slow count of four. Hold that breath for another count of four, then exhale through your mouth for a third count of four.
- **Lazy 8 breathing.** Place your finger in the middle of a figure 8 in the air and begin slowly tracing it with your finger. As you move around one side of the 8, breathe in, and as you move to the other side, breathe out.
- **Cookie breathing.** Picture yourself holding a freshly baked cookie. Breathe in through your nose to smell the chocolate chips or vanilla, then blow out to cool down your treat.
- **Dinosaur breathing.** Take a deep breath before releasing it with a dinosaur roar.

Question Your Thoughts

To learn and think; to think and live; to live and learn, this always, with new insight, new understanding, and new love.

—Sylvia Plath

The thoughts we think project out into the world and affect our perception of it. If you have a negative perception of anything or anyone, you can choose to change your mind. Perception is a result, not a cause. When we judge others, we are imposing our own limiting beliefs on what we perceive. Accept that everything you know is provisional and that there is much you don't know and aren't aware of. That rude driver who cut you off and ran a red light might be taking his wife to the emergency room. That student who tells you he hates you might have seen his dog get hit by a car.

Practice

Today, notice the judgments you make about others that are based on only part of the picture. Be aware of how often what you think may not be accurate. Also be aware that our thoughts and words have a significant effect on how our lives unfold.

Student Connection

Share this scenario with students: When Lucy gets on the bus, she waves at a friend sitting in the back, but her friend doesn't return the wave. Ask students what Lucy might infer from this experience. After discussing, share some possibilities. Perhaps Lucy's friend didn't have her glasses on, or maybe she was distracted looking out the window. The objective here is to notice how we often personalize situations and make inferences that are not based on enough information.

Mind Management

Life management begins with mind management. The quality of your life is influenced by the quality of your thoughts. Your thoughts do form your world.

—Robin Sharma

Mind management is a skill that can be learned. If our minds are full of negative thoughts, our mental and physical health both suffer. Though we may not be able to control the events of our lives, we can learn to control our responses. If someone whispered in your ear the negative thoughts that *you* think about yourself, you probably wouldn't put up with it.

Practice

If we put a quarter of the time we spend caring for our bodies into caring for our minds, we'd see a dramatic decrease in mental health issues. By practicing mental hygiene, we can learn to engage the inner self-observer who notices when we are participating in negative thought patterns. Then, we can reframe our thoughts and train our minds to be gentle with ourselves, look for the good, and replace criticism with compassionate wisdom.

Student Connection

It's never too early to explain to students about cognitive distortions. A *cognitive distortion* is an irrational thought or belief that causes a person to perceive reality inaccurately. We can unknowingly reinforce these thoughts and beliefs over time. One such distortion is overgeneralization, which is taking an isolated negative event and turning it into a pattern of loss and defeat. For example, a student who does poorly on a spelling test might say, "I *always* fail; I'll never learn to spell." Another common distortion is catastrophizing, which means jumping to the worst possible conclusion in every scenario, no matter how improbable. You can spot this because it usually begins with a "what if" question: "What if I fail the next test? I might flunk out of school!"

Sara Olsher's *Don't Believe Everything You Think* (2022) is a perfect book for exploring with students the twisted world of our thoughts.

Creative Visualization

The story you tell yourself determines your reality—change your story, change your life.

—Tony Robbins

In her book *Creative Visualization*, Shakti Gawain (2010) talks about using your imagination to create a clear image, idea, or feeling of something you wish to manifest. If we took the time to envision what we really want, we could create a life that dissolves the problem of time and makes our day-to-day existence profoundly more meaningful. Gawain emphasizes the importance of regularly practicing visualization to manifest goals.

Practice

Develop a clear image of what you want to achieve. Feel the emotions associated with the desired outcome. A study at the University of Colorado at Boulder (2018) found that when you imagine something, your brain activates the same neural pathways as when you actually experience it, which can speed up the learning of new skills.

Student Connection

Conscious movement of the muscles around the eyes helps reinvigorate the surrounding tissues as well as the eyes themselves. In addition to helping with circulation and flexibility, these stretches help relieve eye strain (Gupta et al., 2020). Have your students follow these steps:

1. Briskly rub your palms together until warm.
2. Cup your palms over your eyes. Feel comfort and warmth while breathing softly.
3. Remove your palms from your eyes.
4. Look way up and then way down. Repeat. Look diagonally way up to the right and then diagonally way down to the left, then look diagonally up to the left and diagonally down to the right. Repeat.

Tell students they've now warmed up their ability to visualize.

Read aloud a book with a detailed description of the setting and have them visualize what it would be like to be there. *Owl Moon* (Yolen & Schoenherr, 1987) is my personal favorite for this activity.

Analysis Paralysis

An hour of planning can save you 10 hours of doing.

—Dale Carnegie

Analysis paralysis refers to the state of overanalyzing a situation to the point that a decision never gets made. Every decision we make during the day depletes our energy and our willpower, so it's best to minimize in-the-moment decisions, plan ahead, and follow through with our plans to ensure a productive and successful day.

Practice

Consider implementing the Sunday Meeting Self-Care Plan, a process I wrote about in *Practicing Presence* (Lucas, 2017). Set aside 30 minutes on Sundays and follow these steps:

1. Review your calendar. Once you see your calendar in front of you, you may realize how little free time you have.
2. List in red any nonnegotiable appointments you have this week.
3. Schedule your top two personal priorities for the week. For example, I reserve two hours a day for exercise and meditation. Seeing just how much time you need to accommodate priorities can be life-altering.
4. Plan what time you will go to sleep. This may sound like overkill, but it's important. The only time I can find to exercise is 5:00 a.m., which means I have to go to bed by 9 the night before. Part of self-care is getting on a schedule and restoring some of your energy reserves.
5. Identify how much time after work you need to prepare for the following day. I usually schedule 30 minutes of uninterrupted time to do this.
6. Using your favorite-colored ink, write in a weekly mini-retreat that you promise to do for yourself. Mine have included hiking at the arboretum, spending time reading, and baking my favorite dessert.

Student Connection

Tell students they have 10 minutes to each create a paper airplane. Provide them with paper, scissors, and plenty of open space as well as some simple directions. When time is up, have the students line up and all throw their airplanes at the same time. Note the various designs and the different trajectories. Afterward, talk with students about the importance of making decisions and have them discuss their decision-making process for creating the paper airplane.

Could I Be Wrong?

The secret to being wrong isn't to avoid being wrong! The secret is being willing to be wrong. The secret is realizing that wrong isn't fatal.

—Seth Godin

We obviously tend to think that our beliefs and attitudes are correct; if we didn't, we wouldn't have them. But the truth is, most of us are more confident than we should be. Marshall and colleagues (2013) found that people regularly overestimate their abilities, knowledge, and beliefs. Overconfidence is not only the most pervasive bias that plagues our thinking but also the most catastrophic, often leading to calamitous decisions.

I used to have a "wrong jar" in which I'd keep slips of paper that recorded incidents when my husband was certain that he was right and turned out to be wrong. I have since recognized that keeping the wrong jar was, ironically, as wrong as my husband was in those recorded instances, and I would not recommend this to anyone.

Practice

Practice intellectual humility: the understanding that we can't fully trust our beliefs and opinions because we might be relying on faulty or incomplete information. Be open to the possibility that you don't have the whole picture. Before settling on a belief, listen to alternative perspectives with an open mind, and be willing to entertain new information.

Student Connection

When your students proclaim a strong belief in something, encourage them to seek further information and alternative perspectives. We want our students to be open-minded.

Hold debates about current topics in class as a way to highlight contrasting perspectives.

Get a New Playlist

Music gives a soul to the universe, wings to the mind, flight to the imagination, and life to everything.

—Plato

Recently I was immersed in my same old solitary routine at the gym when I heard the song "Happy" by Pharrell Williams blasting from the bicycle spin studio. Uncharacteristically, I wandered in and hopped on a bike, joining a class already in progress. For the next 30 minutes, song after song uplifted my mood, making me realize that I needed a new playlist. The instructor generously shared hers with me.

Like songs on an old playlist, the thoughts in our heads also tend to repeat over and over until they're stale. Notice the thoughts that you tend to revisit, and see if you can change your mental playlist.

Practice

Create a new music playlist as a reminder that you need to change your internal soundtrack as well.

Student Connection

Collaborate with your students to create a new "playlist" of activities for the morning routine. Mix up your morning circle time, start the day outside doing jumping jacks to upbeat music, use sidewalk chalk to practice math facts, or bounce a ball to some phonemic awareness rhymes.

No Complaining

Keep your thoughts positive because your thoughts become your words. Keep your words positive because your words become your behavior. Keep your behavior positive because your behavior becomes your habits. Keep your habits positive because your habits become your values. Keep your values positive because your values become your destiny.

—Mohandas Gandhi

If you listen carefully to the conversations around you, you may find that complaining is often a central theme. Complaints are often conversation starters, and complaining about how busy we are is practically a badge of honor. We bond together over how overworked and exhausted we are.

Practice

Try *not* to complain for seven days. Wear some type of band on your wrist; every time you complain, you have to switch the band to the other wrist and the clock starts over.

Jon Gordon offers the following strategies to curb complaints (slightly modified here) in his book *The No Complaining Rule* (2008):

- Take a long deep breath before you speak.
- Be aware of the words you use.
- Notice your thoughts and reframe the negative thoughts you think.
- Monitor your self-talk and your internal meanderings.
- Notice the words others use. Start tuning in to the language you hear.
- Judge less; accept more. Look for the good in others and their actions rather than mistakes.
- Envision those who are annoying you as small children in a sandbox waiting for their turn for the shovel.
- Practice gratitude. Take in the good, and record it if possible.
- Decide whether you want to be right or be happy.
- Decide what's worth complaining about. Intentional complaining is better than mindless complaining.

Student Connection

Have a "no complaining" challenge for one day in your classroom. You could put students in teams, give each team a bucket and chips, and have them put a chip in every time someone in their group complains. At the end of the day, have each group count the chips. The group with the fewest chips wins.

No Gossiping

Gossipers are terrorists because with their tongues they drop a bomb and then leave, and the bomb they drop destroys reputations everywhere.

—Pope Francis

Every conversation you have can either drain or fuel you. Gossip is a poisonous form of communication that can negatively affect any kind of relationship, whether it's between friends, family members, or coworkers. It drains time and energy and decreases productivity. In my leadership coaching courses, we learned that organizations with a culture of gossip often have higher turnover rates because most people don't want to deal with the drama.

People tend to gossip about others to make themselves feel better, but the opposite usually happens. Davidson (2012) explains that the subconscious mind can't tell the difference between something negative we say about others and negative talk about ourselves.

Practice

Gossip is a quick and easy way to bond with people, and it's highly contagious, so this practice might be challenging—but it's well worth trying. Choose not to join in gossip. If you're around someone who's criticizing someone else, wait until they're done and counter with something positive about the same person (e.g., "I know you think Jules puts on airs, but I have found that he is an incredible listener who has supported me many times"). Reframing gossip like this typically stops the gossiper in their tracks—but be prepared, as you may not be included in the gossip next time.

Student Connection

The nursery rhyme "Sticks and stones may break my bones / But words can never hurt me" is absolutely not true: More than 160,000 kids stay home from school every day in the United States to avoid being bullied (Gillians & Cooper, 2022). Teach your child or students that the very best way to stop gossip and bullying is to never, ever start it or spread it.

Possibilities, Not Limitations

Nothing is impossible—the word itself says "I'm possible"!

—Audrey Hepburn

We underestimate how many possibilities we have to learn new things, especially in the age of the internet. Very seldom do we face a problem that someone else hasn't already figured out. If we have the desire to learn, the information is at our disposal.

Practice

Think about something that you don't know how to do but would like to learn and do some research. For example, I want to have some raised vegetable gardens in my backyard, and I have found countless tutorials on the subject online. I have also reserved books at the library on gardening and discovered old magazines on gardening at the antique store. My cousin, a gardening expert, has become my mentor on the subject. The possibilities are endless.

Every month, think of one new thing you'd like to learn. Start looking for resources to support your new learning. You'll be amazed at how much help shows up once you take action.

Student Connection

Place your students in groups and have them work on a task that you know would be a challenge for some, but easy for others. For example, you could have them build a structure out of playing cards. Balancing cards on top of one another is not easy, and it becomes more difficult as you build up the cards and they get higher. Or you can give them marshmallows and wooden toothpicks and challenge them to build the most creative structure they can; afterward, have each group describe what they made. The intent is to teach students to ask for and offer help and acknowledge that they all have different strengths.

Every month, ask students to list one new thing they would like to learn. Have them generate a list of resources (people, books, etc.) they can access for support.

Responding Rather Than Reacting

When you react to a person's negative comments or actions in an angry, overly emotional or aggressive way, then you are giving that person power over you. If a person can easily get a rise from you, then you are no longer in control. If you take a moment and respond in a calm, healthy, honest, and real way, then you are in control. You are not allowing anyone to take your power away or invoke a reaction from you.

—Maria Consiglio

Look for opportunities to be nonreactive. Put others at ease by offering peace and ease freely, knowing that what you put out into the world cycles back into your life. Practice responding from a place of presence rather than reacting from a place of stress.

Practice

Here's a three-step process to help you practice nonreaction:

1. **Pay attention.** You know what negativity looks, feels, and sounds like, so be on the lookout for it. If you see it coming, you have a chance to stand back and pause before reacting. Make a conscious choice not to engage with the negativity you encounter.
2. **Recognize it's not about you.** Remind yourself that other people's negativity is a reflection of something going on inside their own minds and being projected toward you. Too often, we get tangled up in other people's negativity because our egos take their words personally.
3. **Wish others peace and ease.** Silently wish those who are being negative peace and ease. Distance yourself if appropriate.

Student Connection

Explain to students that their breath is like a remote control they can use to pause before responding to someone's negative comment. Tell them to take two deep inhalations and exhalations before responding to a negative comment.

Let the Morning News Go

I'm not interested in TV much. I quit watching the news a couple years ago, and my outlook on life has gotten a whole lot better.

—Tom Petty

If you're one of those people who watches the news first thing in the morning or last thing at night, I strongly suggest replacing it with something more uplifting. Listening to a litany of accidents, weather disasters, deaths, and political turmoil will not improve the world, and the mental images they provide can stay with us throughout the day or disrupt our rest at night.

Practice

Although it is important to be aware of what is happening in the world, we can be intentional about the source of the news we consume and the amount of time we spend consuming it. As a former journalist, I want all citizens to be informed, but with accurate information and moderation. The 24-hour news cycle is too easily accessible for many. Think of much of the news and social media as a drain on your life and replace it with positive pastimes. These might include movement, meditation, reading, journaling, listening to an uplifting podcast, sitting outside and listening to the world wake up—anything other than filling your mind with negativity.

Student Connection

Television and social media can influence how students think and behave. When they are chronically exposed to violent content, for example, they may become desensitized. Even technology innovators such as Bill Gates and Steve Jobs have admitted to limiting their children's onscreen time because of the violent content that is aired (Clement & Miles, 2017). In *Screen Schooled*, Clement and Miles observe that Silicon Valley parents seem to grasp the addictive powers of smartphones, tablets, and computers more than the general public does, despite the fact that these parents often make a living by creating and investing in that technology. Nevertheless, media literacy is more important than ever, so as educators, we need to teach students how to determine whether news sources are reputable and savvily navigate contemporary media even as we limit students' daily exposure to screens. We can share with parents the danger of watching unmonitored sensationalized news reports on television and consuming skewed information on social media.

Paternalistic Lies

Is there anyone who has never, ever lied? I wonder.

—Author unknown

I lied to my mother. I said her doctor wanted her to go for physical therapy for a week or two, until her balance was better. Meanwhile, we dismantled her beautiful townhouse and tried to make her single room at the assisted living memory unit facility look like her home. It didn't, and deep down, I know she knew. Yet she never questioned me; she just looked sad. Is it ever OK to lie? I'm not sure.

Practice

Day-to-day life presents what comedian Jerry Seinfeld called "must-lie situations." These are situations in which people lie because they think it is the ethical or kind thing to do. Some call these well-intentioned lies "white lies," but there is another, more pointed, name for them: *paternalistic lies*. Often, we tell paternalistic lies to spare others' feelings. However, doing so requires us to assume we know what is in the recipient's best interest, which is presumptuous and can backfire (Lupoli et al., 2018). And are we truly telling these lies to protect others or to protect ourselves?

Personally, I'm still not sure if there are cases when it's OK to lie. I have met others who say that lying for any reason is unethical and honesty is always the best policy. Talk with your friends, family, and colleagues to see what they think. You might be surprised at what you hear.

Student Connection

Have students pretend to decline a birthday party invitation from a classmate by saying, "I'm sorry, I can't make it" without adding a fib.

Today I'll Play the Victim Again

If you always play the victim, you'll always be the victim.

—Steven Aitchison

Some people remain trapped in the role of victim—they've rehearsed the lines for so long that they don't even have to practice anymore. It just comes naturally. With a trained ear, you can detect self-victimization in seconds.

The opposite of self-victimization is self-responsibility. We are all responsible for our lives—period. Being helpless doesn't get us what we need. We can lean on others for support, but in the end we need to stand on our own. A victim mentality causes us to overlook the good things in life.

Practice

A victim tends to blame others or external circumstances for their predicament. When you are feeling self-pity about something, ask yourself, "What is my role in this situation?" Another good question is "If everything has a purpose, what can I learn from this?" A victim tends to think the current bad situation may never end and prays for it to be over. Instead, search for the strength to be OK in any situation.

Student Connection

Students who see themselves as victims will often catastrophize; words like *never* and *always* are prevalent in their descriptions of their circumstances. They may say things like, "People are always mean to me" or "I never get invited to parties." Our role is to help change their perception. For example, you might ask them, "Is it absolutely true that people are *always* mean to you or that you *never* get invited to a party?" Teach them to question their thinking and gradually change their self-perception of victim.

Snowball Thinking

When you overthink, you originate obstacles that never existed.

—Amit Kalantri

Remember: Where your attention goes, your attention grows. Do you ever take a small thought and catastrophize it by turning it from a "snowflake" to a "snowball"? We can easily go from "I forgot to respond to that parent's email" to "That parent will contact the principal, which will lead to my being reprimanded, and all the other parents will know, and so will my peers, so I may need to transfer schools. I am an idiot."

Practice

When you hear yourself starting to engage in snowball thinking, notice it and slow it down. Catch yourself catastrophizing before your thoughts spiral out of control. Now talk to yourself like you'd talk to a friend, replacing your inner critic with a caring coach-like voice that is reasonable and has your best interest at heart.

Student Connection

Give your students a slightly negative scenario and have them write what they think will happen next. For example: "You wake up late, don't have time to eat breakfast, and miss the bus." Students might add things like "You get grounded" or "Your mom gets fired because she had to drive you to school" or "You lose your best friend because they sat with someone new on the bus." Next, have students crumple their papers up into "snowballs," form a circle, and toss the snowballs into the air. Each student then picks up someone else's snowball and reads it aloud in turn. After each student reads, lead a class discussion about how our minds easily run wild and how most "snowball thinking" never comes to pass.

8

Presence

Presence begins at home and continues in the workplace. Being present can make a difference in your personal life, in your instructional practice, and in the lives of your students. This chapter provides practices to do before you enter the classroom so you can flow through the day feeling calm rather than overwhelmed. Think of these practices as anchors that prevent you from being carried away by the endless waves of ever-changing demands of the classroom. You can use the student connections to teach learners to tune in to presence—a key ingredient in cognition and growth.

Paths to Presence

The most precious gift we can offer others is our presence.

—Thích Nhât Hạnh

There are so many paths to peace and presence—and they all lead to a similar feeling—but each path is unique. Let's accept that we each follow different paths to peace and presence. My husband fly-fishes and writes music. My Buddhist friend chants. My mom used to spend hours gardening. My daughter makes floral arrangements. My colleague walks in the woods. All of these are pointers toward presence.

Practice

What are you doing when you feel most present? Notice what brings you peace. Can you find time to do more of it? Is there a new practice you'd like to "try on" to see if it brings you peace? Vow to find an activity that resonates with you (you can try some in this book!) and brings you into the present moment.

Student Connection

Children often seem present when focused on their technology. Although it's important for children to develop an aptitude for technology since they will be using it in their school and work lives, too much of it can affect their physical, personal, and social development (Turner, 2021). As with most things, a healthy balance is key.

Take your students outside on a nature walk to find large rocks. Have each student paint their rock. If possible, create a stepping-stone path outside your classroom that reminds them to be present as they enter the school.

Presence Pause

At any moment the fully present mind can shatter time and burst into NOW.

—Brother David Steindl-Rast

How often do you pause during your day to see if you are truly present? How can you even remember to do this? One way is to set a timer. Twenty-five-minute intervals of focused work would be optimal.

Practice

Have you ever noticed that you hold your breath when you sit down at your computer to answer emails? Most people do the same thing—they forget to inhale or take shallow breaths after logging on to their computers. Psychologist Linda Stone calls this state *email apnea.*

To stay calm and clearheaded as you work through those emails, try simply exhaling for twice as long as you inhale. Try it right now. Pause to ask yourself if you are breathing, then take a break to inhale, exhale, and stretch. Or simply take a deep sigh every time you click on a new email. Believe it or not, sighing is good for us!

If you incorporate presence pauses into every day, you'll reap the benefits. This is a dose-responsive practice, meaning the more frequently you do it, the better you'll feel and the more you'll remember to do it again.

Place visual reminders (e.g., a sticky depicting the pause icon) to breathe in places where you find yourself getting easily frustrated or stressed (e.g., on your desk, in your kitchen).

Student Connection

Pauses in the form of wait time before and after asking students questions is a longstanding strategic teaching move. I tend to inhale to the count of four, then exhale to the count of four. Everyone processes questions and answers at different rates, and generous wait time ensures you'll find more students volunteering to answer with more thoughtful responses.

Place stickers that remind students to take a presence pause in various places around the classroom: on tablets, on the windows, at their centers, on the board, and so on. Be creative. You can even have students choose the locations. During some of these pauses, you can lead students in a breathing exercise (inhale to the count of four; exhale to the count of four; repeat for a total of four times).

Forgive Freely

Forgiveness is a virtue of the brave.

—Indira Gandhi

Some of us seem to catalog all the perceived wrongs we've accumulated over the years; it's as though we have a storehouse of negative memories that we find some pleasure in accessing. As long as you are remembering the perceived wrongs done to you, you will never be completely free to grow and move forward in your life. It is therefore primarily for your own benefit that you should forgive others. Forgiveness is your path to freedom.

Forgiveness is also a huge step on the path to presence. Most of our negative thoughts focus on either the past or the future. In this present moment, we have a clean slate.

Practice

Follow the L^4 strategy for dealing with perceived slights—look, lean, learn, and let go:

1. **Look** at the perceived slight objectively. If you bury it, it will subconsciously hold you back.
2. **Lean** into the feeling it provokes.
3. Ask yourself what you can **learn** from the situation—both the perceived slight and the feeling it provoked.
4. **Let** it go. Sincerely and completely forgive others—as well as yourself, for holding on to the negative feeling.

Student Connection

Have students print the name of a person they wish to forgive or a situation they wish to move on from on a piece of paper. Have them **look** at how they were hurt. Encourage them to remember how they felt at the time and to **lean** into that feeling. Then, have them consider what they might have **learned** from that event. Ask students to form a circle and put a trash can in the middle. If they wish, they can opt to read their entries one at a time. Finally, everyone crumples their papers and **lets** go of their perceived wrongs by tossing them into the trash can.

Optimism and Presence

The positive thinker sees the invisible, feels the intangible, and achieves the impossible.

—Winston Churchill

Imagine it's a year from now and you've been incorporating presence into your life every day. You've slowly built a mindfulness practice and, unbelievably, you no longer dread meditating. In fact, you look forward to it. At first it was a minute, then two, and now you've worked your way up to 15 minutes per day. You awake every morning with a sense of optimism and gratitude for another day. You begin your day by thinking of what you can look forward to. You've learned to appreciate the simple things in life, and it doesn't take much to make you feel grateful. That feeling of being overwhelmed has disappeared. Throughout the day, you feel a sense of inner peace. When things don't go well, you simply pause and thoughtfully respond rather than overreact. You think of encounters with a challenging colleague as opportunities to practice presence. You feel well equipped to navigate the difficulties of daily life.

Practice

I found this paragraph in a note that my Aunt Anne sent to me. She had typed it on a piece of beautiful paper. I discovered that it was paraphrased from a poem by Dr. W. Heartsill Wilson (1954), a motivational speaker. The words are worth remembering:

Remember, this is the beginning of a new day. You have been given this day to use as you will. You can waste it or use it for good. What you do today is important because you are exchanging a day of your life for it. When tomorrow comes, this day will be gone forever. In its place is something that you have left behind. Let it be something good.

Student Connection

We don't always intentionally close the school day. It just ends; backpacks get packed, coats retrieved, buses called, and we miss an opportunity to reflect. Set aside 10 minutes to have a closing circle. Encourage students to share three good things that happened today.

What's Important Now?

Your goal is not to battle with the mind, but to witness the mind.

—Swami Muktananda

Grasp fully this moment, and only this moment. Living fully in the present is a learned behavior. To develop this skill, make every effort to keep your mind on what is happening in the present moment.

Practice

What you are doing right now is what's important. Give your full attention to one thing. Let the thoughts that distract you slip away. Don't follow them. But don't get frustrated if your mind wanders, either—today is about noticing how untamed our minds are. Do your best to acknowledge your unproductive thoughts and let them pass without getting lost in them.

Whatever you are doing, just do it. If you are wiping the kitchen counter, just wipe the counter. Feel your arm move, notice the smell of the cleaner, see if you can focus on just the task. Notice how it feels to finish.

Student Connection

Knowing there's a limit to how long they must direct their attention to something can make it easier for students to stay focused. Set a timer for how long your students need to work before taking a break. Increase the amount of time gradually as their attention improves. You might even have them graph their improvement. For younger students who have a more difficult time focusing, consider providing a reward at the end of multiple timed focus sessions. This will help students feel more motivated and support their concentration.

Accept This Moment

Accept—then act. Whatever the present moment contains, accept it as if you had chosen it. Always work with it, not against it.

—Eckhart Tolle

Accept this moment as if you had chosen it. Ultimately, it's how you respond to the moment that matters, because that's the only thing you can control. Stop looking back and regretting. Forget obsessing about what the future will bring. Instead, do your best with what you have right now.

Practice

All of us have made pivotal decisions that guide the trajectory of our lives. When I look back on my life, I realize all the different choices I could have made and what a different life would have followed. Matt Haig's *The Midnight Library* (2020) is a good fiction book that explores the concept of the multiple lives we could have lived if we had chosen differently.

Student Connection

Have your students role-play or brainstorm the different ways that they could respond to the following simple scenarios.

- Your parents went away for the weekend and you're at home with your grandparents.
- You lost something important that you were specifically cautioned to take good care of.
- You missed the class field trip because you were sick.
- Your friend came over, but it didn't turn out to be the day you had planned.
- Your pet passed away and your friend won't stop talking about how awesome their pet is.

After the role-playing, grant students time to reflect on how the various responses made them feel, and the fact that there are no single right or wrong responses, but simply options.

Bells of Peace

Peace is liberty in tranquility.

—Marcus Tullius Cicero

May there be peace in your heart, in your home, and in the world. I use sights and sounds in my everyday environment as reminders to pause, breathe in, breathe out, and tune in to the present moment. Even the buzzer that goes off when I forget to fasten my seat belt in the car has changed from an annoying sound to a cue for me to be present. Something as basic as sunlight reminds me to return to the present, breathe, and slow down.

Practice

Whenever I am teaching at the university, I make use of the bells to practice presence and peace. When the clock bell rings outside our lecture hall, I stop talking, and the students and I close our eyes and listen intently to the beautiful sound. (I am sure most students think it sounds better than my lecture.) The first time we did this, I explained to students that they could simply listen, or they could send peace to themselves, to the people they love, to the people they struggle with, and to those they don't know well but who need prayers of peace.

Student Connection

Instruct your students to use school bells as an invitation to pause and send peaceful intentions to the people they love, to the people they've met but aren't close to, to their classmates, and to all beings around the world. Drawing their attention to bells can help encode the sound in their minds as a cue to be present.

Perfect Timing

If we could untangle the mysteries of life and unravel the energies which run through the world; if we could evaluate correctly the significance of passing events; if we could measure the struggles, dilemmas, and aspirations of mankind, we could find that nothing is born out of time. Everything comes at its appointed moment.

—Joseph R. Sizoo

If we could truly get behind the idea that everything that happens in our lives occurs at precisely the right moment, we would save ourselves a lot of time worrying about the future. We'd also realize that we can deal with anything the world throws at us. We'd stop trying to control everything and realize we don't have the big picture, and we're not meant to.

Practice

The next time you're at a red light, take a deep breath, exhale, and enjoy the brief pause. We are constantly going, always thinking about what is left to do. Be grateful for the red lights in your life. The light turned red at the perfect time—to give you a moment to pause.

Student Connection

Have your students describe a time when they encountered someone at the perfect time. Perhaps it was a friend, teacher, or parent. Perhaps they showed up somewhere and something positive happened at that moment. Have them reflect on that experience.

Have your students play kickball outside. Before the game, instruct them to notice all the aspects of the game that are dependent on timing: the kicking and catching of the ball, stealing bases, knowing when to run and when to hold. It's a great metaphor for life.

What You Resist Persists

What you resist not only persists, but will grow in size.

—Carl Jung

So much suffering is increased when we resist what is; so much relief, release, and peace are possible when we simply accept the present moment. Feelings are felt in the present moment. The sooner we can accept a feeling, the sooner we can move on to a new one.

We waste our time, expend our energy, and make things harder by resisting, repressing, and denying. Instead of repressing a thought or feeling, think it, feel it, then release it. Thoughts are temporary and changeable. Resistance and repression will not change a thing. What's repressed can make us depressed. When we accept what is and who we are in the present moment, we are able to change and grow.

Practice

Contemplate the meaning of acceptance. The opposite of acceptance is resistance. What you resist persists.

Notice the resistance you feel. Sometimes resistance feels like an internal struggle between two parts of ourselves—one that overtly wants to process uncomfortable feelings and another that wants to repress them.

Student Connection

As teachers, we need to validate our students' feelings. Tell them it's OK to feel what they're feeling. Often what students want more than anything is for their feelings to be affirmed, so don't try to distract them or make them feel better by making little of their feelings.

When a toddler has a surge of emotion, it erupts, and then, just as quickly, it's over. This is how feelings are meant to pass through us—like waves in the ocean that rise, crash, and subside.

Mindfulness Misconceptions

Mindfulness isn't difficult, we just need to remember to do it.

—Sharon Salzberg

Mindfulness isn't about becoming good at sitting silently on a meditation stool and eliminating our thoughts. It is about learning new ways of being in the moment by responding, rather than reacting, to everything that life brings our way. It's about noticing the most mundane moments. When we are mindful, we connect with others more authentically because we notice them more intentionally.

Practice

Do you notice the constant stream of thoughts whenever you try to sit still and quiet your mind? If so, you are practicing mindfulness. Can you commit to two minutes a day of stillness, to slowly build this practice? There are loads of meditation apps available—I use the Calm app (http://calm.com) to meditate and the Insight Timer (https://insighttimer.com) to track the duration and frequency of my practice—but you certainly don't require one.

Student Connection

Learning meditation at an early age will help students realize that they can train their minds and avoid succumbing to the tendency to judge, label, evaluate, analyze, and comment on everything. A gentle way to introduce mindfulness to students is to begin with belly breathing. Have them follow these steps:

1. Lie down with a favorite stuffed animal beside you.
2. Place your hands to your sides and keep your legs straight.
3. Be still and gently close your eyes.
4. Let your body relax; pretend you are melting into the floor.
5. Put your stuffed animal on your belly.
6. Slowly breathe in. As you fill your belly with air, notice that your animal goes up.
7. Slowly breathe out. As your belly goes down, so does your animal.

Use It or Lose It

We must use what we have to invent what we desire.

—Adrienne Rich

If we don't exercise our muscles, they waste away. If we don't exercise our minds, they begin to close. If we don't use our gifts, we have trouble discerning our purpose, making us depressed and draining us of our creative edge and energy.

Practice

Are you in touch with your natural gifts? Do you use them? Just because we're good at something does not mean that's what brings us joy. We often have gifts that lie dormant because we've lost our true selves trying to live up to others' expectations. Today, try tuning in to notice whether you are utilizing your natural gifts.

Student Connection

The best way to identify a student's gifts is to watch where they invest their energy unprompted by adults. When do they seem most alive, most present, most absorbed? What are some of the things they enjoy doing at school or talking about with you or their peers? Nurture these interests gently, without pushing. Sometimes we don't connect the dots and we miss what is right in front of our eyes. I spent years wondering what vocation my son would choose. He eventually became an architect. When he was younger, he'd move the furniture around in his room all the time and spent hours building with blocks and sketching. The dots were right in front of me; I just didn't connect them.

Slow Down

This is the time to be slow.

—John O'Donohue

Remember who won the race between the tortoise and the hare. We make mistakes when we go too fast. Why are we always in such a rush? Is it possible to slow down? Why does it feel like there are never enough hours in the day?

Practice

Today, notice your pace and try to decrease the speed. Drive, walk, talk, even breathe a bit slower. Notice how this makes you feel inside.

Student Connection

Students have a tendency to rush, especially when completing a task they don't like. Timers in the classroom can help. We often think of timers as ways to limit time, but you can also use them to mark the *minimum* amount of time students need to complete a task. You might even issue students "speeding tickets" if they are moving too fast.

Have students record the time they start an assignment and the time they finish it, explaining that you expect them to spend a minimum amount of time working. If they finish early, they should use that time to enhance their work.

Last Day on Earth

Forever is composed of nows.

—Emily Dickinson

A former colleague of mine spent his last year of work counting the days till retirement. When the day finally came, he had a massive heart attack on his way to breakfast.

Don't spend your time counting the days until something happens. None of us knows if we'll be here tomorrow, so the best thing we can do is to live every day as if it were our last on Earth.

Practice

Pretend it's your last day on Earth—the last time you'll hug someone good-bye; your last breakfast, lunch, and dinner; the last time you'll see the sky. Doesn't that change your perspective?

For a longer practice, imagine you've been given a year to live and list what you would do in that time. Examine your list. How many of those things are you doing now?

Student Connection

Have students design their perfect day, from start to finish. Create a timeline template and have them illustrate or label the activities they would do on their perfect day.

Missed Opportunities

Opportunity is missed by most people because it is dressed in overalls and looks like work.

—Thomas Edison

Most of us can look back and realize that our lives have been full of missed opportunities. It helps to think about them as lessons that we missed but that will come back around when we're ready. Regrets don't help—but learning from our missed opportunities does.

Practice

Our classrooms are full of missed opportunities. A robust conversation is taking place, all are engaged, and a student adds something unexpected. But because the teacher is not listening for an opportunity to delve deeper, they simply say, "Great. Who's next?" or "Interesting. Does anyone else have a question?" When students speak, pause, be in the moment, see if the input is valuable, and engage.

Real listening is an art, and most of us would be well served to listen more and talk less. If we go into class discussions aiming to synthesize students' comments rather than just get through the content, we will increase the value of the conversation.

Student Connection

Students often hold back on joining in or trying something new because they feel unsure of themselves. Instead of having them focus all their energy on what they already excel at, encourage your students to diversify. Attaining new skills makes kids feel capable and confident that they can tackle whatever comes their way.

Teach your students a game they can play on their own, like Solitaire. Such games build confidence, challenge students to make strategic decisions independently, and provide them with a sense of achievement. They also make a great reward for students who finish their classwork early.

Cherish the Ordinary

There have been many articles about the top regrets that people have when they're dying. They are always, "I missed the ordinary moments." We miss those ordinary moments, and yet, that's what we're trying to distract ourselves from at the same time.

—Geneen Roth

When I look at my old photo albums and videos, I find they are often heavy on holidays. Birthdays, Halloween, Easter, and Christmas seem to be captured year after year, followed by sporting events and the occasional vacations. But what I yearn for are memories of the ordinary. I find myself scrutinizing the most mundane photos, zooming in on a shot of the old yellow telephone on the wall, my grandmother's half-full teacup, the faded flowered wallpaper.

Practice

Today, take photos of the ordinary moments: the breakfast dishes, the unmade bed, the sleeping child, your spouse's morning hair, the tree outside. Mark this day on your calendar, and every year spend this day capturing the ordinary. When you or your family look back years from now, they'll have a feel for what your life was really like.

Student Connection

Have your students create a video of an ordinary day. Or, if this isn't an option, have them compose a breakfast-to-bed story that describes each aspect of their day (including illustrations).

Be Here Now

Stopping the endless pursuit of getting somewhere else is perhaps the most beautiful offering we can make to our spirit.

—Tara Brach

"Be here now" is a phrase made famous by the Harvard psychologist turned spiritual teacher Ram Dass. Nothing could be simpler, right? Where else would we be? And yet, in no time we start worrying about an upcoming deadline or reflecting on the curt comment our spouse made, and we are either zooming off to the future or spinning in the past—nowhere near here.

Practice

We're missing out on life if we're living in our heads rather than connecting with the immediacy of being alive. For 10 minutes today, see if you can bring yourself back to here and now. What do you notice about your mind? Does it seem wild and unruly? That's normal. Recognizing this wildness is the beginning of taming it.

Focusing is a practice of being mindful of our felt experience. It offers a parallel to the practice of mindfulness. Whereas mindfulness directs you to bring yourself back to an anchor (often your breath), focusing allows your mind to center on the internal felt sense of your body.

Student Connection

Conduct a "humming focus" activity. Tell students that you're going to practice taking a deep breath through your nose and, as you exhale, you'll make a humming noise. Demonstrate this practice, focusing on the feeling of your throat, mouth, and forehead as you hum. Next, put your hands over your ears and notice how the sound changes in your ears. Finally, lead students through the same focusing practice.

Seeing the Signs

Sis, pay attention to the signs. Sometimes it is exactly what it looks like.

—Author unknown

After my dad died, I would run on a trail by a lake near my home. At one spot on that trail was a straggly old maple tree. For some reason, I would stop and look at this one leaf hanging on an otherwise bare branch and tell myself that as long as the leaf was there, my dad was looking out for me. Crazy, I know. But grief does crazy things to us. Or maybe not so crazy—maybe the signs we give meaning to are real and are sent to us when we need them most. That leaf hung on through fall, winter, and spring. Even as new buds appeared, that leaf clung to the branch.

Practice

Today, expect guidance and be receptive to signs. Don't doubt them, just accept them. Don't dismiss coincidences as being insignificant. Tune in. Be open to possibilities. Pay more attention to what you are experiencing. Don't get in your own way by questioning any signs that appear. Even if you don't believe the signs were "sent" to you, just recognizing them yourself can be enough.

Student Connection

Guide your students to look for signs. You are helping them stimulate their imagination, focus their mind, and bring their full attention to the present moment.

Pointers Toward Presence

Your presence is the most precious gift you can give to another human being.

—Marshall B. Rosenberg

You can feel presence. When you yourself are present, you are fully attentive, engaged, engrossed, and embodying the moment. When your body is there but your mind is absent, others can feel it: the energy feels scattered, frenetic, and fragmented. This book is full of pointers toward presence. Each day is an invitation to enter the present moment.

Practice

Presence can be your default way of being. You know you are becoming more present if you find yourself on autopilot less often and more prone to saying the right thing at the right time.

To practice presence, pick an activity that you typically do on autopilot and vow to be fully aware and present when you engage in it. For example, if you are driving, feel your hands on the steering wheel, feel the seat beneath your legs, notice the temperature and the subtle sounds inside the car. Be present to the physical aspects of driving. That's a far cry from listening to the radio or a podcast, looking out the window, or talking on the phone, all of which are distractions.

Student Connection

Take your students on a field trip to a dog park and encourage them to notice how in-the-moment the dogs are. Any conflicts are quickly forgotten; they are fully present, not ruminating or worrying but simply being.

Just Breathe

Learn how to exhale, the inhale will take care of itself.

—Carla Melucci Ardito

Anxiety and deep breathing cannot coexist. During moments of increased stress, we tend to take very shallow breaths. Deep breathing quickly calms the body and mind.

Practice

If you find yourself worrying, try diaphragmatic breathing. Basically, this means breathing from your belly rather than your chest:

1. Put one hand on your chest and the other on your stomach.
2. Breathe in slowly through your nose, focusing on filling up your belly with air.
3. Notice the hand on your chest stays still while the one on your stomach rises.
4. Exhale through your mouth, feeling the hand on your stomach return to its original position.
5. Repeat for several minutes until you notice the calming effect.

Student Connection

Guide your students in 7-11 breathing: inhaling to the count of 7 and exhaling to the count of 11, then repeating three times. You can provide a visual, such as a Hoberman sphere that expands when they breathe out and contracts when they breathe in. Or have them use their hands, with their fingers touching to open and close.

9

Routines and Rituals

What's the difference between a routine and a ritual? We don't often closely examine our routines; they are like unconscious habits that we engage in to get things done—necessary but not always meaningful. Rituals, by contrast, have more significance and are more emotionally charged. Sometimes what begins as a routine can become more imbued with meaning and evolve into a ritual.

This chapter prompts you to examine the "why" of the routine actions you take, bringing your attention to your home and classroom habits and providing ideas on how to establish healthier routines and rituals for you and your students.

Fuels and Drains

What drains your spirit drains your body. What fuels your spirit fuels your body.

—Caroline Myss

As the first assignment in my Social-Emotional Learning for Adults college course, I have students submit an action plan based on a survey of the "fuels and drains" in their life. This survey is a tool I designed years ago to use when coaching clients. The idea is that you can't add more presence (fuels) into your life until you eliminate the things that are exhausting your time and mental energy (drains). This means setting clear boundaries. Change begins in small increments, so the plan is to focus your attention on eliminating one drain and adding one fuel at a time.

Practice

Make a list of the drains in your life. Choose one to eliminate and a fuel to replace it. Here are some examples:

- *Drain:* Checking emails after 7:00 p.m.
- *Fuel:* Using evenings to prep meals for the week
- *Drain:* Bringing work home
- *Fuel:* Reading a book for pleasure

Student Connection

Have students make collages of the fuels and drains in their lives. They can draw or cut and paste pictures of things that make them happy and of things that make them feel not-so-good. Older students can write about why they chose the pictures they did. Each week, have students try to eliminate one drain and add one fuel.

Plan a Mini-Retreat

Going on retreat is a time to cocoon so that we may emerge ready to return to our lives with a new perspective.

—Anonymous

We tend to think of a retreat as an extended period where we go away and restore ourselves. However, there are all kinds of ways to retreat. A mini-retreat can be as simple as retreating from the routine of everyday life. Maybe you explore a new place to hike, or you stop by a coffee shop you've never been in, or you go to a movie by yourself.

Practice

Open your calendar, look at the week ahead, and pencil in an hour that you are going to set aside just for you. I like to use a code so no one knows that hour is for me—my calendar has a standing weekly meeting with Sophie (i.e., a retreat with myself).

Student Connection

Teach your students the joy of spending time alone doing exactly what they want to do. Make them aware they don't always need a friend or a formal activity to find joy. Help them explore ways they can retreat and restore at an early age. Build into your class schedule short increments of free time during which they can explore an activity they enjoy doing on their own.

Note It

Brain extenders are anything that gets information out of our heads and into the physical world: calendars, key hooks by the front door, note pads, "to do" lists.

—Daniel Levitin

Put a notebook in the kitchen.

Profound, right? I know, ridiculously simple and perhaps a bit outdated. However, sometimes old-school does the trick. Here's the rationale: So much happens in the kitchen. You're listening to an author being interviewed and want to remember his name, or watching a cooking show and want to record the ingredients, or talking with a friend who mentions a great new Netflix series. Buy yourself a spiral-bound notebook (with a hard cover that can be easily wiped clean when you drip coffee or spaghetti sauce on it), and place it somewhere accessible in the kitchen.

Practice

Keep a hardcover spiral-bound notebook that you can attach a pen to. Ease is the goal here. This will become your memory keeper, journal, and record of daily life. Consider sketching as well as writing. I also keep a notebook in the car—it's perfect for recording ideas I hear on podcasts or the titles of songs I want to add to my playlist.

Student Connection

We want to encourage students to learn to record what they need to recall or do. Their memories are more acute than ours, but they tend to remember only what's important to them. Assign each student a "note it" partner to share notes with at the end of the day, including their system for noting what the homework is, upcoming due dates, and other important things. You can also teach them some simple strategies for sketching notes. A great book about this is *The Sketchnote Handbook* (2012) by Mike Rohde. Students will appreciate learning how to use images to capture key concepts, which makes note taking more creative and fun.

Seamless Rituals

Rituals are not fixed—they are constructed and reconstructed over time, to fit people's needs.

—Gleb Tsipursky

Do your rituals change depending on the season? Do you enjoy a cup of hot coffee under a quilt before diving into your day during the chilly winter months, but prefer a glass of water with lemon on the front porch during the warmer months? Notice how your rituals change depending on your mood as well.

Practice

Take time to reconstruct one of your rituals, even if it's as simple as seasonally changing the scent of a candle or diffuser oil.

Student Connection

Ask your students to share one activity they love doing after school. Having students share their established rituals provides opportunities for connection and helps generate ideas for how they can meaningfully spend their time. Enlist their input about what new ritual they would like to incorporate into their school day. Brainstorm ideas on chart paper and have students put sticky notes next to their top three choices. Try each ritual for a week, and then have everyone vote for which one your classroom will adopt for the rest of the month or season.

Decluttering

Clutter is nothing more than postponed decisions.

—Barbara Hemphill

Why is decluttering so emotionally fraught? When I moved, I purged more than half of our possessions. Although it felt freeing to clear things out, I also felt a sense of loss. I gave away my mom's artificial Christmas tree, my Nikon camera, and boxes and boxes of books.

When our environment is cluttered, our minds feel cluttered. When we take the time to donate or discard what we no longer use, we make space for what we value most. You can trust that something new will emerge in the newfound space.

Practice

It's often easier to keep track of items that we don't have duplicates of. For example, when I have multiple pairs of scissors, I can never seem to find them. If I have just one, I'm able to locate it every time.

Donate duplicates. Take some things out of a room in your house and notice how much more you value what remains.

Student Connection

Explain to students that a messy desk contributes to a messy mind, while an organized desk creates space both in the desk and in the mind. Designate one day a week when students clean out their desks. Have the "desk fairies" inspect the desk and give clean desk awards.

Consider giving students a homework assignment to clean or organize a space in their home and take before-and-after pictures. Allow time for reflection and sharing.

Eight Minutes of Clearing

Create the space and a bigger life happens.

—Alysia Reiner

Often the space you clear is more valuable than what is in it. Clutter is distracting and draining. It can be physical or mental: Too much stuff is physical clutter; rampant thoughts, unconscious beliefs, and unhealthy habits are mental clutter. The latter leaves little space in our minds for envisioning, dreaming, and creating.

Practice

Every day, set a timer for four minutes to clean up some of the physical clutter in your home. Just as important, be sure to also give yourself a minimum of four minutes a day to simply breathe and clear the clutter from your mind. In just eight minutes, you will very quickly find yourself reaping the rewards of a less cluttered household and a less cluttered mind.

Student Connection

Make it a habit for your students to spend four minutes a day organizing and cleaning their desks. Micro-habits like this can help students stay ahead of their clutter before it becomes overwhelming—and it's a life skill that will serve them well for years to come.

A great visual to help students better understand how their minds can become cluttered is a glitter jar. You can also use a glitter jar to explain how the brain works: When emotions are rising, your brain (the jar) floods with cortisol (the glitter), reducing its flexibility and reasoning capabilities. As you breathe, the cortisol dissipates (the glitter settles at the bottom of the jar), your brain clears, and you feel calmer, allowing you to make better decisions. Just the act of shaking a glitter jar and watching its contents settle is calming, so carve out a few minutes for this activity. You can find a recipe for making glitter jars at https://heartmindkids.com/how-to-make-a-glitter-jar-for-mindfulness.

Habit Stacking

How we spend our days is, of course, how we spend our lives. What we do with this hour, and that one, is what we are doing.

—Annie Dillard

One of the best ways to build a new habit is to "stack it" onto an existing one. For example, I want to start drinking my green juice in the morning before I consume anything else. An existing habit I have is taking my vitamins every day after I exercise. If I bundle having my morning juice with taking those vitamins, I'm stacking the new one onto the old one.

In his 2018 book *Atomic Habits*, James Clear recommends asking the following four questions about any habit you want to maintain:

1. How can I make it obvious?
2. How can I make it attractive?
3. How can I make it easy?
4. How can I make it satisfying?

Practice

Identify a new habit you'd like to adopt. Brainstorm habits you already have in place and see if any can be used for stacking the new habit. Then, decide when and where would be best to implement the habit.

Student Connection

If you want your students to read more books, stack the habit of reading onto something they are already doing every day. For example, you could make independent reading a part of their morning routine. Have books displayed around the classroom each morning. After students unpack and greet their peers, invite them to participate in a book walk, find a cozy spot, and read for five minutes. They can then summarize what their books are about during circle time. Adding a bit of accountability and giving them the opportunity to share help build community.

Keep the Routine Going

Fake it until you make it.

—Steven Tyler

Often, when we're feeling down, we stop our normal routine. This unfortunately frees up time for our brain to torment ourselves with negative thoughts. Abandoning our routines only exacerbates any low feelings and delays us from getting out from under the fog. A routine helps our brain form established neuropathways, enabling us to engage in that routine regularly without having to consciously bully ourselves into submission to keep it up. The more we do something, the smoother and wider these pathways become, which makes the routine easier to access.

Practice

Today, keep up with your normal routine. Stop obsessing about whatever is bothering you. Sometimes you can "fake" your way into a better way of thinking and feeling.

Student Connection

Many children thrive on routines. The expected helps them feel stable, and they appreciate the continuity of a day that feels familiar. What positive routines can you keep as a constant in the classroom? Model the importance of creating time each day to do small things that make you happy.

On your daily schedule, list the first task as "me time" for students. When they first arrive in class, encourage them to take a mindful moment, write down one thing they're grateful for, and stick it in a class "gratitude jar." Then, have them select from several "me time" activities (e.g., mindful coloring, building with blocks, working on a puzzle). After they've engaged in the chosen activity, have them journal about what they enjoyed about their "me time" that morning.

Use Your Spare Moments

Guard well your spare moments. They are like uncut diamonds. Discard them and their value will never be known. Improve them and they will become the brightest gems in a useful life.

—Ralph Waldo Emerson

Spare moments can be productivity gold mines. Utilizing small two-minute increments to get things done can have amazing effects. Almost any task begins with small steps, and any forward motion is better than stagnation.

David Allen, author of *Getting Things Done* (2002), suggests doing any task that can be done in two minutes immediately. This is a great trick that ensures you'll at least do *something* productive each day.

Practice

Every evening, take two minutes before you go to bed to organize a space in your home in preparation for the next day. You'll find waking up to an organized space helps start the day off on a positive note. Look for two-minute pockets of time during class to organize your desk. It is amazing what can be accomplished in two minutes.

Student Connection

Our students need unstructured time; we don't want to fill every moment with things they have to do. However, having them take two minutes to organize a classroom center is teaching a skill that will be a lifelong asset. At the end of the day, set a timer for two minutes. Put some music on, and have everyone straighten, organize, and clean up an area in the classroom.

Curb Your Compulsions

*The secret to permanently breaking any bad habit is to love something greater than
the habit.*

—Bryant McGill

Sometimes when I get that anxious feeling in my chest, my mind goes into worst-
case scenario mode, and I binge-eat my feelings. But when I become aware of
that sticky habit that feeds the fire of anxiety, I am able to replace it with something healthier.

Practice

Put a sticker of a pause button on the refrigerator or wherever else your
"sticky habit" tends to reside—maybe your wallet, if you tend to shop when you're
anxious, or your phone, if you're a scroller. You want some type of visual cue to
slow you down before you begin your anxiety-fueled mindless binge. Then think
of something healthier but still pleasurable to replace your habit.

For example, I used to indulge in a Diet Coke every afternoon for a quick
pick-me-up. Wanting a more nutritious alternative, I swapped the soda for a cold
green tea–herbal tea blend. I experimented with brands and flavors, and now I
look forward to and savor my afternoon tea. A sticky habit turned into an enjoyable ritual.

Student Connection

It's never too soon to teach children how to slow down and savor their food.
Give each student half a grape and lead them through the following prompts:

1. Examine the grape from all angles. What do you notice?
2. Now, smell the grape. Does it have an aroma?
3. How does the grape feel with your fingers? Is it warm or cold? Is it smooth,
   rough, or sticky?
4. Put the grape on your tongue, but don't chew it yet. Leave it on your
   tongue and notice how it feels in your mouth. Do you taste anything yet?
5. One bite at a time, slowly start chewing the grape. Notice how the taste
   changes as you chew.

This practice teaches students how to focus all their attention on just one
thing, without distractions. They are learning to direct and sustain their attention. They are learning to be fully present.

Idle Practice

If you are idle, be not solitary; if you are solitary, be not idle.

—Samuel Johnson

I'm not often idle; in fact, people are constantly encouraging me to slow down. There is value in taking a little time to let our minds wander and daydream. Occasional idle time can improve both focus and concentration, helping us to approach problems with renewed clarity, as well as provide an opportunity for creative thought and reflection.

Practice

Create an "idle list" where you list things you can do that fall under the category of pure leisure (this means nothing work-related!).

Student Connection

Once a month, give your students an idle afternoon. Put out the clay, watercolors, games—anything without a screen. Encourage students to bring something from home that they'd like to share. School can be incredibly stressful, and it's often hard to find time to just sit and think—yet it's during these moments of quiet reflection that we often come up with our best ideas. Students should come back to academic time feeling refreshed and ready to learn.

Practice What's Right

Wisdom is not gained by knowing what is right. Wisdom is gained by practicing what is right and noticing what happens when that practice succeeds and when it fails.

—Barbara Brown Taylor

I don't always know what the right thing is. But I try. If you know what you value and have a strong internal compass, you can usually feel if something is right. When I was a school administrator, I had to make countless decisions, and they weren't always popular. I made those decisions every time based on what I believed was best for students. Whether about curriculum, report cards, or staffing, the only way I could make decisions was knowing that I was there to be an advocate for students first.

Practice

Model "doing the right thing" for your students. As educators, doing the right thing comes down to what's in the best interest of the students in your class. Throughout the day, just do the right thing. For example, when confronted with a colleague or parent who wants to gossip, don't engage. When a colleague needs help, be supportive. Your students are watching and listening to you more than you might realize. Standing up for what's right can inspire your students to take similar actions. A great deal of teaching isn't telling but showing.

Student Connection

Read the book *Do Unto Otters* (Keller, 2007) to your students. This book highlights how to be a good friend and neighbor by following the golden rule. After reading the book, create a T-chart with columns labeled "I would like others to" and "So I will." Brainstorm ideas with students of things they would like others to do and that they should do as well. Discuss with students that doing the right thing has a reciprocal effect.

Keep It Simple

Simplicity is about subtracting the obvious and adding the meaningful.

—John Maeda

The ability to take complex ideas and make them easy to understand is a sign of a great teacher. Students appreciate simple instructions and clear language, and their parents appreciate candid, jargon-free communication. In everyday life, nature teaches us that profound beauty often lies in simplicity—think of a single flower in a vase.

Practice

Simplify your phone. Delete old contacts and unused applications. Purge your texts. Change your lockscreen to something simple. Update your wallpaper to something that makes you smile.

Student Connection

Many students want to be constantly entertained. They never want to be "bored." As educators, we know sometimes being bored can be a wonderful thing, providing time for creativity and imaginative play.

Find 10 minutes today for students to engage in unstructured imaginative play. Provide blocks, tiles, and other building tools and watch what students can do. Even better, if you have large boxes, put students in groups and have them create forts.

The Fine Line Between Rhythm and Rut

Choose your rut carefully.... You'll be in it for the next 150 miles.

—Sign along an Alaskan highway

Though we sprinkle vacations, holidays, and celebrations in between, most days are pretty mundane. In his 2012 book *The Power of Habit*, Charles Duhigg describes the "habit loop" like this:

> This process within our brains is a three-step loop. First, there is a cue, a trigger that tells your brain to go into automatic mode and which habit to use. Then there is the routine, which can be physical or mental or emotional. Finally, there is a reward, which helps your brain figure out if this particular loop is worth remembering for the future. (p. 19)

We can use the concept of the habit loop to make our daily lives have more of an intentional rhythm and feel less like we're in a rut.

Practice

Decide who you want to be and then create a rhythm of daily habits that support your vision. Want to be a writer? Wake up and write. Want to be more in shape? Vow to find a way to move your body that you enjoy. Want to live simpler? Commit to giving something away any time you buy something new. Want to meditate? Set a timer reminding you it's time to meditate and track your progress.

Routinize the essential. We are what we repeatedly do.

Student Connection

Most children thrive on routine and predictability. Consistent routines provide them with a sense of safety—but there is a difference between rhythm and a rut. For example, once students know the days of the week and the months of the year, it can be more than a little boring to go over them in morning meeting day in and day out. For more information about this, check out the article "Calendar Time for Young Children: Good Intentions Gone Awry" by Beneke and colleagues (2008).

The Pomodoro Technique

Sit, relax, breathe.... There are 1,440 minutes in one day, so taking 5 of those minutes to re-energize will not be the end of the world.

—Author unknown

The 80/20 Rule states that 80 percent of output comes from 20 percent of input. Keep this in mind throughout your day. For example, when you notice yourself randomly clicking or scrolling mindlessly on the computer, stop. Just as having multiple tabs open slows down your computer and productivity, having multiple things on your mind slows your ability to focus and find clarity. It's time to get out of your head and back into your body: Go for a walk, stretch, change the clothes in the dryer—anything to stop the mindless clicking.

Practice

Commit a certain window of time every day exclusively to sifting through email. I usually set aside 24 minutes. During that time, only answer emails. You will notice distractions tempting you to switch to something else. Pull yourself back from temptation and stay on task. You will achieve more in less time. Once the time is up, give yourself a few minutes to move away from the computer and reenergize.

When I am grading papers, writing, or doing any task that will take an extended time, I often use the Pomodoro technique (Cirillo, 2018). I've modified the steps here:

1. Identify a task that you need to complete.
2. Set a timer for 24 minutes.
3. Work on the task you identified with no distractions.
4. When the alarm sounds, take a 4-minute break.
5. Repeat the process four more times.
6. Take a longer 10-minute break and start the process again.

Student Connection

Establish "focus challenges" in your classroom. You can have students use a modified version of the Pomodoro technique to help them choose tasks to do in a certain time window.

Challenge yourself to notice when students are starting to lag and lose steam. Drop everything and transition to some type of movement break. Rather than having movement breaks planned into your schedule, use them when it is clear your class needs them. A movement break can be as simple as playing Simon Says or stretching or, if you have time, running a lap around the school.

Recovering a Sense of Possibility

With Morning Pages, we serve as a witness to our own experience, listening to ourselves each morning and thus clearing the way for further listening throughout the day. With Artist Dates, we listen to the youthful part of ourselves who craves adventure and is full of interesting ideas. And with Walks, we listen both to our environment and to what might be called our higher power or higher self—I myself, and my many students, have found that solo walks consistently bring what I like to call ahas.

—Julia Cameron

We are all creative; every single soul has something inside that is waiting to be expressed. Sometimes it gets covered up by the need to wash the dishes, make the bed, shop for groceries, clean the house, pay the bills, and tend to the endless laundry. But inside there is a nagging feeling that you should be doing something more. If you want to recover that sense of possibility, consider Julia Cameron's 1992 book *The Artist's Way: A Spiritual Path to Higher Creativity*. In it, she recommends three consistent practices: Morning Pages (i.e., journaling), Walks, and Artist Dates.

Practice

Today, find a journal and a pen that allow you to write quickly. They don't have to be fancy; I've found a spiral notebook allows me to not feel the pressure of writing something profound. Write about anything that crosses your mind, just be honest and authentic. Next, find the time to take a solo walk for at least 20 minutes. Finally, schedule an Artist Date: a meandering outing like a browse through an antique store, a drive to a lake, or a wander through a bookstore—anything that inspires you.

Student Connection

Teach your students to wonder, question, and ponder possibilities. Foster their curiosity, which enhances their imagination. Ensure they have time for creative activities like drama, crafts, music, and dance. Have a class play, a poetry celebration, or daily dance parties. Don't let anything cover up the endless possibilities they have to be innovative and creative.

A Morning Greeting

How glorious a greeting the sun gives the mountains!

—John Muir

One of the participants in a mindfulness course I teach wrote these words in a journal:

> Many things have stood out for me during this course. The first was that too many of us just go through the motions in our daily life and neglect to take the time to stop and see what is in front of us. Everyone you talk to seems to exude a level of stress, and in education there seems to be a level of negativity and burnout more than ever. The stress seems to overtake the ability to be truly present. Not being present takes away the importance and gratitude of every day. I thought I was able to hide my emotions fairly well but realize that even [frustration] from a morning meeting may cause my emotions to show to students entering the classroom. If my mind is still attached to a previous frustration, I'm not able to be fully present for students entering each morning. I've made myself step away from my desk each morning and go to the hall to welcome students with a smile. I feel by doing this, I'm more present to their needs. In the classroom, not only do I need to be mindful of my emotions, but model that I am truly paying attention to what students are saying.

Practice

Begin your day by genuinely greeting everyone you encounter. Make eye contact. Smile. Ask a colleague how they are and then give them your full attention.

Student Connection

Challenge your students to say a sincere "Good morning" to as many people as they can. Encourage them to look those they encounter in the eye and see if their smiling face can get others to slow down, pause, and perhaps smile back.

Another option is to teach students jokes to share with those they encounter. For example, "Why did the student eat his homework?" "Because the teacher told him it was a piece of cake." There is something about a child saying, "Knock knock" that brings a smile to almost anyone's face!

10

Self-Care

This final chapter aims to help you create and affirm a
habit of self-care. You'll discover nurturing practices that
you can apply throughout your day. Part of self-care is
taking the time to reflect on *what* brings you joy.

I hope some of the practices will take a permanent
place in your daily life. You can't do everything,
but you can do *something*. The student connections
will help your learners make sensible and
wise choices to support their own well-being.

What Makes You Happy?

Be happy in the moment, that's enough. Each moment is all we need, not more.

—Mother Teresa

It doesn't take much to make me happy: a hug from my husband, my children laughing together, a call from my cousin, watching my granddaughters smiling at one another, hearing a Carolina wren in the spring, feeling the sunshine on my face. I have a sign in my house that says, "These are the good old days."

Practice

As you go through the day, notice the things that make you feel content. Witness how joy can be found in every day. You don't have to plan it. Just notice, experience, and savor the precious moments. Notice the people around you: Do they look happy? Do they act happy? If so, what are they doing? My guess is they are engaging with others.

Student Connection

Ask your students to think about their day. What has made them happy? Then have them all mix around the room. Ring a chime and have them freeze, then share what they thought of with their closest classmate. If they can't think of anything, have them share one thing that would make them happy. You could do this at the end of the day, so students have something fresh in their minds when their parents ask, "How was school today?"

Do We Dare Take Care of Ourselves?

No one can take care of you the way you can take care of you. So, make sure to take care of yourself.

—Dwayne Johnson

Do we really have the right to take care of ourselves? Do we really have the right to set boundaries? Do we really have the right to be direct and say what we need to say? You bet we do. In her 2017 book *Beard in Mind,* Penny Reid tells readers not to set themselves on fire to keep others warm.

Practice

What is being asked of you today? What do you need for yourself? When you make your plans for the day, address your own needs first. You may find you are in a better place to support others as a result.

Student Connection

Have your students nurture a plant. By doing this they learn the value of sustained effort, of doing what is needed, and of being someone who can be counted on. They also learn that caring can make a difference.

Sharpen Your Saw

"Sharpen the saw" means preserving and enhancing the greatest asset you have —you.

—Stephen R. Covey

A man is out in his yard all day trying to cut down a tree with an old, dull saw. A neighbor passing by asks, "Why don't you sharpen your saw blade?" The man replies, "I don't have time for that! I'm too busy cutting down this tree!"

The lesson here is that those who don't make time to sharpen their saw will not be effective, no matter how hard they work.

Practice

How can you "sharpen your saw"? In what areas are you worn down, depleted, or otherwise not functioning optimally? Try to sharpen it. Is it taking care of your body by eating right, exercising, and getting the right amount of sleep? Or do you need to spend more time with family and friends? Maybe you need to learn something new? Identify one area and focus on making changes to it.

Student Connection

Explain the concept of sharpening the saw by having students write first with a dull pencil, then with a newly sharpened one. Have them compare how they wrote with the two pencils. Explain that just as pencils work best when they're sharp, so do our minds and bodies. Share the *SELF* acronym for staying sharp: sleep, exercise, leisure, and food. Have students create a poster using the acronym and add pictures of themselves next to different *SELF* activities. Hang the posters in your classroom as a reminder to students of how to keep their saws sharp.

The 10 Things: A To-Do List for Restoration

We have to start putting ourselves on the to-do list.

—Giuliana Rancic

I usually spend summer and winter breaks catching up on the hovel my house has turned into. I begin every break determined to clean the attic, purge my closet, and organize the piles that have accumulated in the basement.

I'm guessing I'm not alone in becoming a whirlwind of domestic efficiency the minute I get a few days to myself. But perhaps what we really need to do is pause—to take some time to truly restore and do something for ourselves. Not huge things; simple leisure activities like going on bike rides or hikes, discovering new pop-up breweries, taking walks in the snow, catching up on movies, reading a good book in the hammock or by a fire. You get the idea. If you're lucky enough to travel, wonderful, but we don't need to go far from our homes to unwind.

Practice

Open your notebook and create a "10 Things To-Do List." Determine and jot down the following:

- Five things you like to do, the last time you did each one, and an upcoming date when you will do them again.
- Five people you like to spend time with, the last time you saw each one, and an upcoming date when you will spend time with them again.

It's that simple! When we take the time to remember what really brings us joy and who we like to share our time with, we're refueling our empty tanks. We end up feeling rejuvenated, our perspective changes, and who knows? We just might feel like organizing that basement.

Student Connection

Have your students complete their own 10 Things To-Do List. Their responses may surprise you. Challenge them not to include any screens in their list of five things they like to do.

The Necessity of Rest

Almost everything will work again if you unplug it for a few minutes, including you.

—Anne Lamott

When our body signals that we need to rest, we need to listen. Rest is not a luxury —it's an essential part of living a healthy life. When we are rested, we function better and navigate our days with ease.

My daughter, a 1st grade teacher, was nine months pregnant and days away from her due date when she learned that a former student had passed away. She called me and sobbed, "Do you think I could stay home today?" She felt guilty about not going to work. I convinced her to take a mental health day. She cried, rested, reflected, and regrouped. The next morning, she gave birth to her daughter, Lainey Anne—an easy delivery, and a healthy baby. Rest had been a necessity.

Practice

Tune in to your body. When you get the signal to slow down, listen. Those sick days you keep saving are meant to be used, so use them. Overwork and being overwhelmed cause stress-related illnesses. When you are beyond tired, take care of yourself.

Student Connection

Throughout the day, build in short segments of restorative moments for both you and your students to recharge.

Become Acquainted with Yourself

We who live in quiet places have the opportunity to become acquainted with our-
selves, to think our own thoughts and live our own lives in a way that is not possible
for those who are keeping up with the crowd.... In thine own cheerful spirit live.

—Laura Ingalls Wilder

In her powerful book *The Drama of the Gifted Child* (1979), Alice Miller points out that many highly gifted overachievers are driven by a deep-seated chronic depression resulting from their true and authentic selves being shamed through abandonment in childhood. As children, they were loved for their achievements and their performance, rather than for themselves. Their true and authentic selves were abandoned.

Practice

"One is free from depression," writes Miller, "when self-esteem is based on the authenticity of one's own feelings and not on the possession of certain qualities" (p. 34). Notice if you tend to depend on the praise of others. Are you caught in the trap of striving to be recognized for your achievements rather than simply for your authentic self? Is the "real you" missing from your life? If so, it's time to reconnect with the real you. If you're not used to being alone with yourself, this may take some getting used to. Dedicate time each week just for you. Your relationship with yourself is the most important relationship you'll ever have.

Student Connection

Mirroring is the process of reflecting students' authentic selves and accepting them for who they truly are. Today, be a mirror for a student. Be present, acknowledge and take the student seriously, and try to let their real selves feel seen.

Settle for More

If you must compromise, compromise up.

—Eleanor Roosevelt

We get what we settle for. So, if you want more, don't settle for less. You can only settle for less for so long before you start resenting yourself. So, start now. Be direct. Advocate for what you really want. Say what you mean; don't worry so much about other people's feelings. Rock the boat if it needs to be rocked.

Practice

Notice where you settle for less. Think about what it means to settle: surrendering your belief in your own worthiness. A good place to start is by taking stock of your relationships. Today, start examining the interactions you have with your friends at work. The friendships we settle for are those that make us feel drained after every interaction. Set boundaries and stick to them. Distance yourself if that's what you need.

Student Connection

Teach students that they should not settle for just any friend and that friendships are earned by being kind, caring, and supportive. Guide them to understand that friends should trust each other, provide encouragement, and want the best for each other. Although friends may not always agree, they should be considerate of differences.

Ask students if they can think of a pair of good friends in any books, movies, or television shows. Ask how they knew they were good friends.

Make a list of the qualities of good friends on chart paper. Next, have students trace their hand and cut it out (you could precut hands if needed). On the palm, they should print their name. Then, on each finger they should write one trait of a good friend using the qualities listed on the chart. Once finished, each student will have five traits of a good friend listed on their "hand." Have them decorate their hands and display them in the classroom. To close the lesson, have students high-five their classmates and give them genuine compliments.

What the Books We Read Reveal

The reading of all good books is like a conversation with the finest minds of past centuries.

—René Descartes

What you read can be a window into who you are and what you're interested in or passionate about. A friend once asked me what the five most recent books on my Kindle were, and as I recited the list, we both laughed. My books were as divergent as my interests. Each was a window into what I was curious about.

Practice

Look at the last five books you've read. Are the topics varied? Do you tend to read only one genre? Would you benefit from exploring a new subject? If you don't have a library card, get one! You can go online and explore the catalog of options, select some new books, and reserve them. If you're not in a hurry, go wander in your local library and select whatever interests you. By borrowing rather than purchasing, you broaden your choices. Can't get to the library? Download your local library app and borrow books virtually.

A fun and revealing exercise is to answer these book-related questions about yourself:

- If your life were a book, what would the title be?
- What are the chapter titles in the book of your life?
- What chapter are you in now?
- What is the next chapter of your life called?

Student Connection

Instilling a love of reading in students is essential. Take your students to the library and have them each select a book. Once they've done so, take a look at what they picked—it's a lens into interests that they might never have shared before.

Have students answer the list of questions in the preceding Practice section.

Self-Care: The Antidote to Self-Pity

If your compassion does not include yourself, it is incomplete.

—Jack Kornfield

Have you ever noticed how you talk to yourself when you make a mistake? My first reaction used to always be self-criticism; I thought self-compassion was overindulgent, like feeling sorry for yourself, when it's really the antidote to self-pity. According to Neff (2012), self-compassionate people are more likely to engage in perspective taking than to focus on their own suffering. They are also less likely to ruminate on how bad things are, which is one of the reasons self-compassionate people have better mental health.

Practice

Consider the differences between how you treat a friend going through challenges and how you treat yourself. When you make a mistake today, see if you can treat yourself the way you'd treat your friend. Pay attention to your inner dialogue and the words you use. Can you be a bit gentler with and forgiving of yourself?

Student Connection

We want students to be academic risk takers, not to be afraid of making mistakes. Talk candidly with your students about how they feel when they fail at something. Share your own failures and show them examples of others who have failed and then gone on to succeed. Invite your students to research or listen to true stories of some of the world's most famous "failures." Students are often taught strategies to succeed, but what if we spent time modeling strategies for coping with failure? It's often helpful to hear about famous people who have overcome obstacles.

Point out that as humans we share something in common: We all mess up. It's what we do *after* we fail that matters most.

Backdraft

Love reveals everything unlike itself.

—Annie Papatheodorou

Although the intent of self-compassion is to soothe and nurture yourself, some people find that when they practice self-compassion, their discomfort increases instead. This phenomenon is called *backdraft*. It's originally a firefighting term: When a fire is deprived of oxygen, the flames will roar when the door is opened and fresh air is introduced. Something similar can happen when we practice self-compassion: If you're trying to nurture yourself by repeating kind phrases, for example, you may be reminded that no one was there to say those words when you needed them most as a child.

Practice

Pay attention to the feelings that emerge when you practice self-compassion. If you notice backdraft, accept that this is part of the healing process. Little by little, you are learning how to be tender and kind with yourself.

Student Connection

Make a conscious effort to foster emotional intelligence in your students so that they never have to deal with backdraft. Discuss how to care for yourself physically when you're struggling. Teach them how to articulate how they feel and what they need. Can you imagine how much simpler relationships would be if we all learned at an early age to identify how we feel and what would help us feel better?

A simple "Fist to Five" check-in can provide immediate feedback on how your students are feeling:

- Closed fist = Feeling pretty bad
- One finger up = Feeling emotional
- Two fingers up = Could be better
- Three fingers up = Doing OK
- Four fingers up = Feeling good
- Five fingers up = Feeling amazing

Contemplative Reading

Seek in reading and you will find in meditation; knock in prayer and it will be opened to you in contemplation.

—St. John of the Cross

Contemplative reading allows us to slow down and engage deeply and intuitively with the text. It can bring present-moment awareness, and it's a fresh, creative method for reflecting on and cultivating deeper awareness and understanding of the text. It helps counteract the urge to rush through reading.

Practice

Slowly read a passage from a book aloud to yourself. After reading, read it again and highlight anything that speaks to you. Note in the margins (or in a journal if you'd prefer) what this passage makes you imagine or recollect. What resonates with you?

Student Connection

Model contemplative reading for your students. Sit quietly and take a few grounding breaths, then slowly read a poem or an excerpt from a book aloud. When you're done, practice one minute of silence. Next, read aloud a passage or line that stood out to you, followed again by one minute of silence. Have students share a word or phrase in response. Afterward, have students practice the steps you modeled for them with a partner.

Present-Moment Strolling

It is solved by walking.

—Attributed to Diogenes and Saint Augustine

Walking is a great form of physical exercise, and it's also a great opportunity to practice presence.

If you find it hard to be in the present moment, being outside in nature can help. Mindful walking is an easy way to incorporate stillness into everyday life and can be just as effective as seated meditation. Walking can allow your wise self to make an appearance.

Practice

Take a mindful walk in nature today. Notice how your senses can be heightened by being in nature. Tune in to the smells, the sounds, and the visual field. Notice the changing sounds and sights in the world around you as you move. Center yourself and feel the warmth of the sun. Notice the unique scents of the season. Feel the weight of your body every time your foot touches the ground. Flood your feet with awareness. Try to maintain a steady stride. When you finish your walk, stand still and silent for a few moments. Notice the peace and calm in the body. Take that feeling with you throughout the day.

Student Connection

It is always a good time for a nature walk. Give each student a brown bag and have them gather treasures as they walk. The objects they find can be placed in the science center in your classroom. Add a magnifying glass to make it extra fun. You could also have students select a special tree they see on their walk and have them sketch the tree during each season.

Don't Fear Failure

Double your rate of failure.

—Thomas Watson

We can let mistakes and failure take us down, or we can rise above them and learn that failure isn't necessarily a bad thing. We often fail in spite of our best efforts, and the lesson in failure is to begin again.

Practice

We fail the most when we don't try. What are you afraid to do because you think you'll fail?

Student Connection

Many children are accustomed to having their needs met, but do they know how to take care of themselves? Teach students to have realistic expectations for themselves. Explain that mistakes are part of life and are always opportunities to learn.

Have students draw a tree with branches. On the trunk, have them write a mistake they made in the past. On each branch, have them write an outcome of their mistake. The finished product should illustrate that any mistake will have ramifications—some good, some bad, but all forgivable.

What's Next

The way you live your days is the way you live your life.

—Annie Dillard

We don't know what's next. Just accept that. Embrace uncertainty—and do what needs to be done, now.

Practice

If you could have had complete control of your life, would you have learned as much as you have? We spend so much time and energy trying to plan and get it all right when there is no "right." We are in this world to learn and to do the best we can. Show up every day vowing to do your best—that, my friend, is enough, because you are enough.

Student Connection

A concrete way to teach students about uncertainty throughout the year is by keeping an "estimation jar" in the classroom. Each month, fill a jar with small items (marbles, jellybeans, pebbles) and have students estimate the quantity. Once everyone has made their guess, reveal the number and point out that no one was certain about what it would be. As the school year comes to an end, remind them of the jar and that uncertainty is a part of growing and learning. You can also share the following Zen parable about uncertainty to help students think about the transition to a new school year:

> There was once an old farmer who had worked his crops for many years.
>
> One day, his horse ran away. Upon hearing the news, his neighbors came to visit.
>
> "Such bad luck," they said sympathetically.
>
> "Maybe," the farmer replied.
>
> The next morning the horse returned, bringing with it two other wild horses.
>
> "Such good luck!" the neighbors exclaimed.
>
> "Maybe," replied the farmer.
>
> The following day, his son tried to ride one of the untamed horses, was thrown off, and broke his leg.
>
> Again, the neighbors came to offer their sympathy on his misfortune.
>
> "Such bad luck," they said.
>
> "Maybe," answered the farmer.
>
> The day after that, military officials came to the village to draft young men into the army to fight in a war. Seeing that the son's leg was broken, they passed him by.
>
> "Such good luck!" cried the neighbors.
>
> "Maybe," said the farmer. (Muth, 2005, pp. 20–21)

Acknowledgments

I am privileged and grateful to have many wonderful people who have supported me throughout this book project. I want to acknowledge a handful of them here.

My daughter Chelsea LaRose, 1st grade teacher, whose bright light has taught me more about living better days than any research I've unearthed. Chelsea has written, edited, and conducted action research using the practices from this book in her own life and the student connections with her 1st graders.

My cousin and collaborator Jessica Infantino contributed to and helped edit this book and kept believing this project was worthwhile. More important, she showed up when I had not-so-good days.

Bill Varner, a brilliant ASCD senior acquisitions editor who once again believed in me and gave me a chance to publish on a topic that isn't quite mainstream in the world of education.

Miriam Calderone, whose careful editing and creative suggestions made this book considerably better and who made the publishing experience phenomenal.

My husband Andy, who has put up with me hauling a laptop and a bag full of books with me whenever he drives. (I work best when I'm contained, so a car ride is my perfect writing spot.)

My son Craig, whose life is just one better day after another.

My sister Amy, who knows how to listen and support.

Kathy Sweeney, whose authentic friendship means more to me than she'll ever realize.

Jean Fillman, a former kindergarten teacher and friend, who read the entire rough draft and provided insightful ideas and feedback.

My graduate assistant Rachel Schlosberg, who helped brainstorm, organize, and edit.

West Chester University of Pennsylvania graduate students and Garnet Valley School District teachers who conducted action research using the practices and student connections in the book with themselves and their students.

My incredible physical therapist, Chris Coppins, who kept my body healthy so I could work pain-free while writing *Better Days*.

Teachers everywhere, who are doing their absolute best to live better days.

Children throughout the world, who need the adults in their midst to be present and living their best lives.

Divine guidance that is always there, as long as I remember to ask and, more important, listen.

References

Abrams, D., Eller, A., & Bryant, B. (2006). An age apart: The effects of intergenerational contact and stereotype threat on performance and intergroup bias. *Psychology and Aging, 21*(4), 691–702.

Allen, D. (2002). *Getting things done: The art of stress-free productivity.* Penguin.

Behr, G., & Rydzewski, R. (2023). *When you wonder, you're learning: Mister Rogers' enduring lessons for raising creative, curious, caring kids.* Hachette Go.

Beneke, S. J., Ostrosky, M. M., & Katz, L. G. (2008). Calendar time for young children: Good intentions gone awry. *Young Children, 63*(3), 12–16.

Bitsko, R. H., Claussen, A. H., Lichstein, J., Black, L. I., Jones, S. E., Danielson, M. L., Hoenig, J. M., Davis Jack, S. P., Brody, D. J., Gyawali, S., Maenner, M. J., Warner, M., Holland, K. M., Perou, R., Crosby, A. E., Blumberg, S. J., Avenevoli, S., Kaminski, J. W., & Ghandour, R. M. (2022, February 25). Mental health surveillance among children—United States, 2013–2019. *Morbidity and Mortality Weekly Report Supplement, 71*(2), 1–42. https://www.cdc.gov/mmwr/volumes/71/su/su7102a1.htm

Borko, H., & Shavelson, R. J. (1990). Teacher decision making. In B. F. Jones & L. Idol (Eds.), *Dimensions of thinking and cognitive instruction.* Routledge.

Boyd, D. T., Gale, A., Quinn, C. R., Mueller-Williams, A. C., Jones, K. V., Williams, E., & Lateef, H. A. (2023). Do we belong? Examining the associations between adolescents' perceptions of school belonging, teacher discrimination, peer prejudice and suicide. *Journal of Racial and Ethnic Health Disparities, 11*(3), 1454–1464.

Brickman, P., & Campbell, D. (1971). Hedonic relativism and planning the good society. In M. H. Apley (Ed.), *Adaptation-level theory: A symposium* (pp. 287–302). Academic Press.

Brown, B. (2018). *Dare to lead.* Vermilion.

Buscaglia, L. (1982). *The fall of Freddie the leaf.* Henry Holt.

Cai, Y., Yang, Y., Ge, Q., & Weng, H. (2023, September). The interplay between teacher empathy, students' sense of school belonging, and learning achievement. *European Journal of Psychology of Education, 38*(3), 1167–1183.

Cameron, J. (1992). *The artist's way: A spiritual path to higher creativity.* Penguin.

Castel, A. D. (2008). Metacognition and learning about primacy and recency effects in free recall: The utilization of intrinsic and extrinsic cues when making judgments of learning. *Memory & Cognition, 36*(2), 429–437.

Centers for Disease Control and Prevention (CDC). (2023). Anxiety and depression in children: Get the facts. *CDC: Children's Mental Health*. https://www.cdc.gov/childrens-mentalhealth/features/anxiety-depression-children.html

Childre, D., Martin, H., Rozman, D., & McCraty, R. (2016). *Heart intelligence: Connecting with the intuitive guidance of the heart*. Waterfront Digital Press.

Cirillo, F. (2018). *The pomodoro technique: The life-changing time-management system*. Virgin.

Clear, J. (2018). *Atomic habits: An easy and proven way to build good habits and break bad ones*. Avery.

Clement, J., & Miles, M. (2017). *Screen schooled: Two veteran teachers expose how technology overuse is making our kids dumber*. Chicago Review Press.

Cohen, G. L. (2022). *Belonging: The science of creating connection and bridging divides*. Norton.

Collins, J. (2022). *The retrieval routine*. Collins Education Associates.

Csikszentmihalyi, M. (1990). *Flow: The psychology of optimal experience*. Harper & Row.

Dalai Lama, Tutu, D., & Abrams, D. (2016). *The book of joy: Lasting happiness in a changing world*. Penguin Random House.

Davidson, R. J. (2012). *The emotional life of your brain: How its unique patterns affect the way you think, feel, and live—and how you can change them*. Avery.

Dhiman, S. (2007). Personal mastery: Our quest for self-actualization, meaning, and highest purpose. *Interbeing, 1*(1), 25–35.

Dickens, C. (1859/2012). *A tale of two cities*. Penguin Classics.

Docter, P., & Del Carmen, R. (Directors). (2015). *Inside out* [Film]. Walt Disney Studios.

Duhigg, C. (2012). *The power of habit: Why we do what we do in life and business*. Random House.

Emmons, R. (2016). *The little book of gratitude*. Gaia.

English, K. (2024, January 2024). The neurobiology of positive thinking [Blog post]. *LinkedIn*. https://www.linkedin.com/pulse/neurobiology-positive-thinking-kali-english-8zdfe/

Ferlazzo, L. (2021, May 30). The what, why, and how of "interleaving." *Education Week*. https://www.edweek.org/teaching-learning/opinion-the-what-why-how-of-interleaving/2021/05

Ferrari, P. F., & Coudé, G. (2018). Mirror neurons, embodied emotions, and empathy. In K. Z. Meyza & E. Knapska (Eds.), *Neuronal correlates of empathy: From rodent to human* (pp. 67–77). Elsevier.

Foulkes, D. (1999). How to study children's dreams. In *Children's dreaming and the development of consciousness* (pp. 18–39). Harvard University Press.

Fred Rogers Institute. (2022). *Talking with children about difficult things in the news*. https://www.fredrogersinstitute.org/files/resources/7/respondingtodifficultcurrentevents2022.pdf

Fredrickson, B. L., Cohn, M. A., Coffey, K. A., Pek, J., & Finkel, S. M. (2008). Open hearts build lives: Positive emotions, induced through loving-kindness meditation, build consequential personal resources. *Journal of Personality and Social Psychology, 95*(5), 1045.

Gallwey, W. T. (1997). *The inner game of tennis: The classic guide to the mental side of peak performance*. Random House.

Gawain, S. (2010). *Creative visualization: Use the power of your imagination to create what you want in your life*. New World Library.

Geirland, J. (1996, September 1). Go with the flow. *Wired*. https://www.wired.com/1996/09/czik

Gillians, P. E., & Cooper, B. S. (2022). *Keeping school children safe and alive: Strategies to stop bullying and prevent suicide*. IAP.

Gordon, J. (2008). *The no complaining rule: Positive ways to deal with negativity at work.* Wiley.

Gupta, S. K., & Aparna, S. (2020). Effect of yoga ocular exercises on eye fatigue. *International Journal of Yoga, 13*(1), 76–79.

Haig, M. (2020). *The midnight library*. Canongate Books.

Hallowell, E. M. (2015). *Driven to distraction at work: How to focus and be more productive.* Harvard Business Review Press.

Hamilton, D. R. (2017). *The five side effects of kindness: This book will make you feel better, be happier, and live longer.* Hay House UK.

Hammond, J. S., Keeney, R. L., & Raiffa, H. (2015). *Smart choices: A practical guide to making better decisions*. Harvard Business Review Press.

Hanson, R. (2013). *Hardwiring happiness: The new brain science of contentment, calm and confidence*. Harmony Books.

Hemley, R. (2003). *Invented Eden: The elusive disputed history of the Tasaday*. Farrar, Straus & Giroux.

Henkes, K. (2010). *Wemberly worried*. HarperCollins.

John, J. (2022). *The sour grape*. HarperCollins.

Kabat-Zinn, J. (2018, July). A study in happiness—Meditation, the brain, and the immune system. *Mindfulness, 9,* 1664–1667.

Katie, B. (2003). *Loving what is: Four questions that can change your life*. Three Rivers Press.

Katie, B., & Wilhelm, H. (2016). *The four questions: For Henny Penny and anybody with stressful thoughts*. Penguin.

Keller, L. (2007). *Do unto otters*. Henry Holt.

Kiken, L. G., & Shook, N. J. (2011). Looking up: Mindfulness increases positive judgments and reduces negativity bias. *Social Psychological and Personality Science, 2*(4), 425–431.

Kris, D. F. (2017, March 20). The timeless teachings of Mister Rogers. *PBS Kids for Parents*. https://www.pbs.org/parents/thrive/the-timeless-teachings-of-mister-rogers

Lamott, A. (1995). *Bird by bird: Some instructions on writing and life*. Anchor.

Leeb, R. T., Bitsko, R. H., Radhakrishnan, L., Martinez, P., Njai, R., & Holland, K. M. (2020). Mental health–related emergency department visits among children aged <18 years during the COVID-19 pandemic—United States, January 1–October 17, 2020. *Morbidity and Mortality Weekly Report, 69*(45), 1675–1680.

Lowry, D. (1978). *True colors personality test*. True Colors.

Lucas, L. (2017). *Practicing presence: Simple self-care strategies for teachers*. Routledge.

Luks, A., & Payne, P. (2001). *The healing power of doing good: The health and spiritual benefits of helping others*. iUniverse.

Lupoli, M., Levine, E., & Greenberg, E. (2018). Paternalistic lies. *Organizational Behavior and Human Decision Processes, 146,* 31–50.

Luyken, C. (2017). *The book of mistakes*. Penguin Young Readers Group.

MacLachlan, P. (1994). *All the places to love*. HarperCollins.

Madore, K. P., & Wagner, A. D. (2019, March–April). Multicosts of multitasking. *Cerebrum*.

Marshall, J. A. R., Trimmer., P. C., Houston, A. I., & McNamara, J. M. (2013, August). On evolutionary explanations of cognitive biases. *Trends in Ecology & Evolution, 28*(8), 469–473.

Maté, G. (2011). *When the body says no: The cost of hidden stress*. Wiley.

Mead, M. N. (2008, April 1). Benefits of sunlight: A bright spot for human health. *Environmental Health Perspectives, 116*(4), A160–A167.

Mehrabian, A. (1981). *Silent messages*. Wadsworth.

Miller, A. (1979). *The drama of the gifted child: The search for the true self.* Basic Books.

Mindful.org. (n.d.). Loving-kindness meditation with Sharon Salzberg. *Mindful.org.* https://www.mindful.org/loving-kindness-meditation-with-sharon-salzberg/

Mirgain, S. (2020, April 7). *The surprising benefit of going through difficult times.* UW School of Medicine and Public Health. https://www.uwhealth.org/news/surprising-benefit-going-through-difficult-times

Muth, J. J. (2005). *Zen shorts*. Scholastic.

Neff, K. D. (2012). The science of self-compassion. In C. Germer & R. Siegel (Eds.), *Compassion and wisdom in psychotherapy* (pp. 79–92). Guilford.

Neufeld, G., & Maté, G. (2006). *Hold on to your kids: Why parents need to matter more than peers*. Ballantine Books.

Olsher, S. (2022). *Don't believe everything you think: A tale of twisted thoughts.* Mighty + Bright.

Paul, M. (2014, February 4). How your memory rewrites the past. *Northwestern Now.* https://news.northwestern.edu/stories/2014/02/how-your-memory-rewrites-the-past/

Penagos-Corzo, J. C., Cosio van-Hasselt, M., Escobar, D., Vázquez-Roque, R. A., & Flores, G. (2022). Mirror neurons and empathy-related regions in psychopathy: Systematic review, meta-analysis, and a working model. *Social Neuroscience, 17*(5), 462–479.

Pettinelli, M. (2019). *My final analysis of everything—including emotions, feelings and thoughts—by Mark Rozen Pettinelli*. Lulu.com.

Reid, P. (2017). *Beard in mind*. Cipher-Naught.

Responsive Classroom. (2019, September 3). *Setting goals, hopes, and dreams: Connecting students to the community*. https://www.responsiveclassroom.org/setting-goals-hopes-and-dreams/

Rizzolatti, G., & Fabbri-Destro, M. (2010). Mirror neurons: From discovery to autism. *Experimental Brain Research, 200*(3–4), 223–237.

Robbins, M. (Host). (2022, December 12). Three things you need to accept about other people (No. 21) [Audio podcast episode]. In *The Mel Robbins Podcast*. https://www.melrobbins.com/podcasts/episode-21

Rogers, F. (1988). *When a pet dies*. Puffin.

Rohde, M. (2012). *The sketchnote handbook: The illustrated guide to visual note taking*. Peachpit Press.

Rowe, M. B. (1986). Wait time: Slowing down may be a way of speeding up! *Journal of Teacher Education, 37*(1), 43–50.

Saltzberg, B. (2010). *Beautiful oops!* Workman.

Salzberg, S. (1995). *Loving-kindness: The revolutionary art of happiness*. Shambhala.

Sandstrom, G. M., & Dunn, E. W. (2014, July). Social interactions and well-being: The surprising power of weak ties. *Personality and Social Psychology Bulletin, 40*(7), 910–922.

Seuss, Dr. (1940). *Horton hatches the egg*. Random House.

Shannon, D. (1998). *A bad case of stripes*. Blue Sky.

Siegel, D. J., & Bryson, T. P. (2012). *The whole-brain child*. Constable & Robinson.

Stephen, F. A., Ermalyn, L. P., Mangorsi, B. Y., Louise, L. J., & Juvenmile, T. B. (2022). A voyage into the visualization of athletic performances: A review. *American Journal of Multidisciplinary Research and Innovation, 1*(3), 105–109.

Tippett, K. (Host). (2008, February). John O'Donohue: The inner landscape of beauty [Audio podcast episode]. In *On Being with Krista Tippett.* https://onbeing.org/programs/john-odonohue-the-inner-landscape-of-beauty/

Turner, M. (2021). *The negative effects of technology on younger generations* [Unpublished research paper]. Winthrop University.

University of Colorado at Boulder. (2018, December 10). Your brain on imagination: It's a lot like reality, study shows. *ScienceDaily.* www.sciencedaily.com/releases/2018/12/181210144943.htm

Viorst, J. (1971). *The tenth good thing about Barney.* Atheneum.

Viorst, J. (1972). *Alexander and the terrible, horrible, no good, very bad day.* Atheneum.

Wheelan, C. (2022). *Write for your life: A clear guide to clear and purposeful writing (and presentations).* Norton.

Wilde, D. (2013). *Train your brain.* Balboa.

Wilder, L. I. (1943). *These happy golden years.* Harper & Brothers.

Wilson, H. W. (1954). *A new day.* Houghton Mifflin.

Yolen, J., & Schoenherr, J. (1987). *Owl moon.* Philomel Books.

Zander, R. S., & Zander, B. (2002). *The art of possibility: Transforming professional and personal life.* Penguin.

Zwebner, Y., Sellier, A. L., Rosenfeld, N., Goldenberg, J., & Mayo, R. (2017). We look like our names: The manifestation of name stereotypes in facial appearance. *Journal of Personality and Social Psychology, 112*(4), 527–554.

Index

About the Author

Dr. Lisa J. Lucas has more than 35 years of experience in education as a teacher, an instructional coach, an administrator, and a consultant. She is currently a professor at West Chester University of Pennsylvania and a therapeutic coach specializing in stress reduction for professionals. She is the author of *Practicing Presence: Simple Self-Care Strategies for Teachers*. Her vision is to provide professional development to educators worldwide, challenging mental models and inspiring educators and students to navigate a world full of distractions and lost connections by integrating healthy habits into their lives.

A glance into Lisa's car reveals a bit about her personal life. Her calming essential oil and lapis lazuli rock are in the central console. Nearby are a notebook, pen, and library books. Two child car seats monopolize the back seat. In the trunk there might be a yoga mat, bike helmet, kickboard, pickleball racket, hiking boots, beach blanket, or cross-country skis, depending on the season—but there is always a basketball.

Related ASCD Resources

At the time of publication, the following resources were available (ASCD stock numbers appear in parentheses).

The Burnout Cure: Learning to Love Teaching Again by Chase Mielke (#119004)

Educator Bandwidth: How to Reclaim Your Energy, Passion, and Time by Jane Kise and Ann Holm (#122019)

From Stressed Out to Stress Wise: How You and Your Students Can Navigate Challenges and Nurture Vitality by Abby Wills, Anjali Deva, and Niki Saccareccia (#123004)

Make Teaching Sustainable: Six Shifts That Teachers Want and Students Need by Paul Emerich France (#123011)

Mindfulness in the Classroom: Strategies for Promoting Concentration, Compassion, and Calm by Thomas Armstrong (#120018)

The Principal as Chief Empathy Officer: Creating a Culture Where Everyone Grows by Thomas R. Hoerr (#122030)

Rekindle Your Professional Fire: Powerful Habits for Becoming a More Well-Balanced Teacher by Mike Anderson (#124027)

Teach Happier This School Year: 40 Weeks of Inspiration and Reflection by Suzanne Dailey (#123027)

Teaching with Empathy: How to Transform Your Practice by Understanding Your Learners by Lisa Westman (#121027)

Well-Being in Schools: Three Forces That Will Uplift Your Students in a Volatile World by Andy Hargreaves and Dennis Shirley (#122025)

For up-to-date information about ASCD resources, go to **www.ascd.org.** You can search the complete archives of *Educational Leadership* at **www.ascd.org /el.** To contact us, send an email to member@ascd.org or call 1-800-933-2723 or 703-578-9600.